DrawPlus X5 Resource Guide

Contacting Serif

Contacting Serif technical support

Our support mission is to provide fast, friendly technical advice and support from a team of on-call experts. Technical support is provided from our web support page, and useful information can be obtained via our web-based forums (see below). There are no pricing policies after the 30 day money back guarantee period.

UK/International/ US Technical Support:	**http://www.serif.com/support**

Additional Serif contact information

Web:

Serif website:	**http://www.serif.com**
Forums:	**http://www.serif.com/forums.asp**

Main office (UK, Europe):

The Software Centre, PO Box 2000, Nottingham, NG11 7GW, UK

Main:	(0115) 914 2000
Registration (UK only):	(0800) 376 1989
Sales (UK only):	(0800) 376 7070
Customer Service (UK/International):	**http://www.serif.com/support**
General Fax:	(0115) 914 2020

North American office (US, Canada):

The Software Center, 17 Hampshire Drive, Suites 1 & 2, Hudson NH 03051, USA

Main:	(603) 889-8650
Registration:	(800) 794-6876
Sales:	(800) 489-6703
Customer Service:	**http://www.serif.com/support**
General Fax:	(603) 889-1127

International enquiries

Please contact our main office.

Credits

This Resource Guide, and the software described in it, is furnished under an end user License Agreement, which is included with the product. The agreement specifies the permitted and prohibited uses.

Trademarks

DrawPlus is a registered trademark of Serif (Europe) Ltd.

All Serif product names are trademarks of Serif (Europe) Ltd.

Microsoft, Windows, and the Windows logo are registered trademarks of Microsoft Corporation. All other trademarks acknowledged.

Windows Vista and the Windows Vista Start button are trademarks or registered trademarks of Microsoft Corporation in the United States and/or other countries.

Adobe Flash is a registered trademark of Adobe Systems Incorporated in the United States and/or other countries.

Wacom, the logo and Intuos are trademarks or registered trademarks of the Wacom Company, Ltd.

Copyrights

Digital Images © 2008 Hemera Technologies Inc. All Rights Reserved.

Digital Images © 2008 Jupiterimages Corporation, All Rights Reserved.

Digital Images © 2008 Jupiterimages France SAS, All Rights Reserved.

Bitstream Font content © 1981-2005 Bitstream Inc. All rights reserved.

Portions graphics import/export technology © LEAD Technologies, Inc. & Eastman Kodak Company.

Panose Typeface Matching System © 1991, 1992, 1995-1997 Hewlett-Packard Corporation.

The Sentry Spelling-Checker Engine © 2000 Wintertree Software Inc.

PANTONE® Colors displayed in the software application or in the user documentation may not match PANTONE-identified standards. Consult current PANTONE Color Publications for accurate color. PANTONE® and other Pantone, Inc. trademarks are the property of Pantone, Inc. © Pantone, Inc., 2005.

Pantone, Inc. is the copyright owner of color data and/or software which are licensed to Serif (Europe) Ltd. to distribute for use only in combination with DrawPlus. PANTONE Color Data and/or Software shall not be copied onto another disk or into memory unless as part of the execution of DrawPlus.

FontForge © 2000,2001,2002,2003,2004,2005,2006,2007,2008 by George Williams.

Portions of this software are copyright © 2008 The FreeType Project (www.freetype.org). All rights reserved.

Anti-Grain Geometry - Version 2.4 © 2002-2005 Maxim Shemanarev (McSeem)

TrueType font samples from Serif FontPacks © Serif (Europe) Ltd.

© 2011 Serif (Europe) Ltd. All rights reserved. No part of this Resource Guide may be reproduced in any form without the express written permission of Serif (Europe) Ltd.

Serif DrawPlus X5 © 1991-2011 Serif (Europe) Ltd. All rights reserved.

Companies and names used in samples are fictitious.

Screenshots in the Resource Guide are captured from the English (UK) version of DrawPlus.

Introduction

Welcome to the DrawPlus X5 Resource Guide! Whether you are new to DrawPlus or an experienced user, this guide provides content to help you get the best out of the program.

Offering a range of tutorials, along with full-colour previews of DrawPlus's samples. And gallery elements, we hope you'll find this guide to be a valuable resource that you'll return to time and time again.

The Resource Guide is organized into the following chapters:

1: Tutorials

Provides introductory exercises to help new users master the basics, and more challenging projects for experienced users.

2: Gallery

Provides thumbnail previews of the content provided on the **Gallery** tab.

3: Styles

Provides thumbnail prevoews of the preset styles that you can apply with a single click from the **Styles** tab.

4: Brushes

Showcases the categorized natural stroke and spray brushes provided on the **Brushes** tab.

5: Samples

A gallery of examples to illustrate the capabilities of DrawPlus.

Contents

Chapter 1 - Tutorials **1**

Accessing the Tutorials and Sample Files....3

Exploring DrawPlus X5....5

Shapes I: Using QuickShapes....7

Fills I: Solid Fills....13

Brushes I: Using Brushes....21

Gallery....33

Shapes II: Modifying Shapes....43

Fills II: Gradient Fills....57

Brushes II: Spray Brushes....65

Lines: Using the Pen Tool....75

Creating Brushes....91

Text....109

Wax Seal....123

Torn Paper....133

Wine Glass....147

Creating Navigation Buttons....163

Introducing Animation....173

Stopframe Animation....183

Keyframe Animation....189

Chapter 2 - Gallery **203**

Chapter 3 - Styles **297**

Chapter 4 - Brushes **323**

Chapter 5 - Samples **339**

Tutorials

In this chapter, you'll find a selection of illustrated, step-by-step tutorials and projects.

If you're new to DrawPlus, we suggest you work through the tutorials as listed in the Contents.

The earlier tutorials will allow you to experiment with basic creative tools and techniques. Later tutorials will revisit these fundamental DrawPlus tools to provide solutions to creative design challenges. We also explore stopframe and keyframe animation techniques.

Regardless of your current skill level, these tutorials will help you produce great artwork and animations!

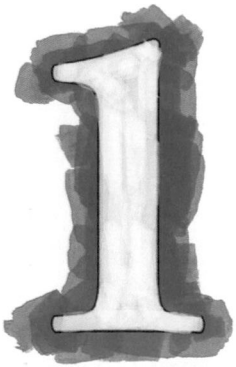

Accessing the Tutorials

You can access the tutorials in one of the following ways:

- From the DrawPlus Startup Wizard, select from the **Learn** section. Different icons indicate the type of tutorial available.

a video tutorial

an online tutorial

see more tutorials and videos!

- or -

- From DrawPlus, click **Help** and then click **Tutorials**.

Accessing the sample files

Throughout the tutorials, you'll be prompted to access sample files. All samples are accessible via the Internet at the following location:

http://go.serif.com/resources/DPX5

If you've clicked on a file, you can either open or save the file. We recommend you save the file to your desktop or a named folder on your computer.

Useful icons

Before we get started, here is a quick guide to the icons that you'll find useful along the way.

When you see this icon, there are project files and/or images available for download that will help you to complete the tutorial. Sometimes we provide you with partially completed projects so that you can concentrate on the main learning point of the tutorial, without having to recreate our design.

Don't forget to save your work! It's good practice to save often. We'll remind you along the way with these helpful save points.

This is a note. Notes provide useful information about the program or a particular technique.

This is a tip. Our tips provide information that will help you with your projects.

This is a warning! We don't want to make you panic but when you see this icon, you need to pay attention to the steps as they will be particularly important.

Exploring DrawPlus X5

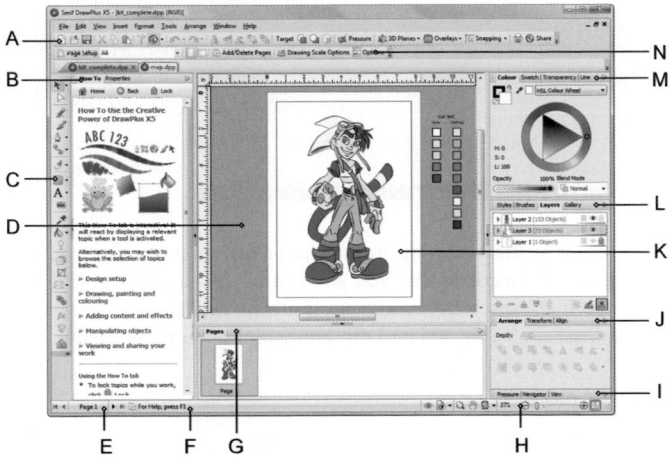

(**A**) Standard toolbar, (**B**) How To & Properties tabs, (**C**) Drawing toolbar, (**D**) Pasteboard, (**E**) Page Locator, (**F**) Hintline toolbar, (**G**) Pages tab, (**H**) View toolbar, (**I**) Pressure, Navigator, & View tabs (collapsed), (**J**) Arrange, Transform, & Align tabs, (**K**) Page area, (**L**) Styles, Brushes, Layers, & Gallery tabs, (**M**) Colour, Swatch, Transparency, & Line tabs, (**N**) Context toolbar.

The DrawPlus workspace

The DrawPlus studio workspace consists of:

- A page area...!
- A surrounding pasteboard area (D), where you can keep elements that are being prepared or waiting to be positioned on the page area. In the example above, we have used this to place our colour reference swatches. This is not displayed when the page is exported.
- Horizontal and vertical **toolbars** and **tabs**, used to access DrawPlus commands and tools.

Move the mouse pointer around the screen and you'll see popup **tooltips** that identify toolbar buttons and flyouts.

Right-click any object or page region to bring up a **context menu** of functions.

Stopframe and Keyframe Animation

When working in these modes, the studio environment updates to display the new tabs and functions that you will need in an easy to use layout. The How To tab is collapsed by default but is always available to open on the left of the Studio. We've outlined the important differences below.

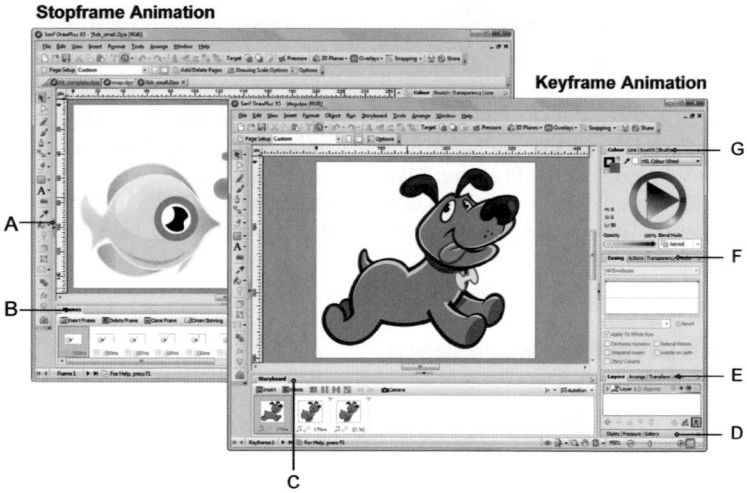

(**A**) How To & Properties tabs (collapsed), (**B**) Frames tab, (**C**) Storyboard tab, (**D**) Styles, Pressure, & Gallery tabs (collapsed), (**E**) Layers, Arrange, Transform, & Align tabs, (**F**) Easing, Actions, Transparency, & Media tabs, (**G**) Colour, Line, Swatch, & Brushes tabs.

Shapes I: Drawing with QuickShapes

In this tutorial we are going to get creative with QuickShapes! DrawPlus has a lot of useful QuickShapes, and with a little imagination, they can be used to create a lot more than a few simple shapes on the page. Let's get started.

By the end of this tutorial you will be able to:

- Draw a simple line using the **Pen** tool.
- Add QuickShapes to a page.
- Use the **Node** tool to edit Quickshapes.

Let's begin...

- In the Startup Wizard, choose **Start New Drawing**, select a page size of your choice and click **OK**.

Drawing a flower

We'll begin by drawing a flower.

To draw a flower stem:

1. On the Drawing toolbar, click the **Pen Tool**.

2. On the context toolbar, click **Smooth Segments** to change the mode.

3. Click once on the page to begin the line, and then, click and drag to create a short, curved line.

4. Press the **Esc** key to finish the line. You should now have a curved line with a start node and an end node.

5. With the line selected, on the **Line** tab, increase the line width to **10** pt.

For more details on creating lines using the **Pen Tool**, see the tutorial *Lines: Using the Pen Tool* on p. 75.

To create the flower head:

1. On the Drawing toolbar, on the QuickShapes flyout, click the **Quick Petal**. Press and hold the **Shift** key while dragging on your page to draw the flower.

The **Shift** key is a really useful modifier key as it constrains the shape proportions. When drawing QuickShapes, it keeps the width and the height equal. Another useful modifier key is **Ctrl**. When pressed, a QuickShape will resize from the centre instead of the corner of the bounding box. Try it and see for yourself!

2. On the **Line** tab, change the line width to **1.5** pt and on the **Swatch** tab, click the **Fill** button and then click the white swatch to fill the shape white.

3. If necessary, re-position the flower head so it is at the top of the curved line. On the Drawing toolbar, click the **Node Tool** and drag the leftmost node upwards until the petals just touch.

4. On the Drawing toolbar, in the QuickShapes flyout, click the **Quick Ellipse**. Press and hold the **Shift** key while dragging on your page to draw the centre of your flower. Re-position it as needed.

To create the leaves:

1. Now for the leaves. On the Drawing toolbar, in the QuickShapes flyout, click the **Quick Heart**. Drag on your page to draw the heart, and with the Node tool, drag the left node down to the bottom.

2. Finally, with the **Pointer Tool**, drag the leaves into position at the base of the stalk. We also rotated our leaves slightly to complete the effect.

That's it! You've drawn a flower using only a single line and a few QuickShapes.

Save now! Click **File > Save As...** and choose a new name for your file.

Why not experiment with the **Quick Petal** nodes to see what other flower shapes you can create using the same techniques? (We'll look at adding colour in the *Fills I: Solid Fills* tutorial on p. 13.)

That's it for part one! In the tutorial *Shapes II: Modifying Shapes* (p. 43) we'll get creative with a **Quick Ellipse** and show you what you can do with this and a few other basic QuickShapes.

Fills I: Solid Fills

Building on the shapes created in the tutorial *Shapes I: Drawing with QuickShapes* on p. 7, we are now going to add a splash of colour.

By the end of this tutorial you will be able to:

- Copy multiple objects.
- Change the colour of lines and fills using the **Swatch** and **Colour** tabs.
- Use the **Format Painter** to copy fill and line properties.

Go to **http://go.serif.com/resources/DPX5** to download the following tutorial project file(s):

quickshapes.dpp

Let's begin...

- On the Standard toolbar, click **Open**.
- Locate **QuickShapes.dpp** and click **Open**. Alternatively, if you have completed the previous tutorials, open the document containing the flower shapes.

Solid colour fills

To begin with we will look at applying solid colour fills to our shapes. For this, we'll introduce the **Colour** and the **Swatch** tab. First, we are going to add colour to a copy of our flower.

To copy objects:

1. With the **Pointer Tool**, click and drag to creating a selection around the flower. On release, the objects are selected.

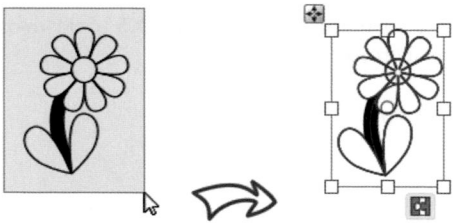

2. Hold the **Ctrl** key and drag the selected objects. (Release the mouse button before the **Ctrl** key to complete the copy.) On release, the new objects are selected.

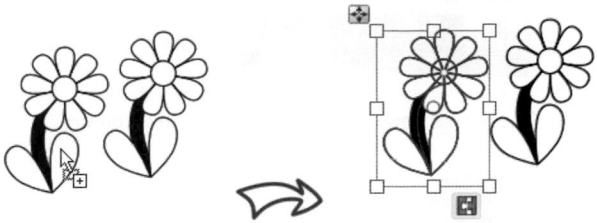

If the **Ungroup** button is displayed beneath any of your objects, click it to ungroup the elements before you change the colour of the lines and fills.

To apply a solid fill and line colour (Swatch tab):

1. With the **Pointer Tool**, click to select the petals.

2. On the **Swatch** tab, the **Document Palette** is displayed.

   - Click the **Line** button and then, click a dark blue swatch.

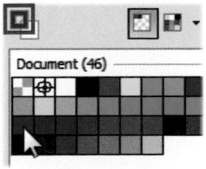

- Click the **Fill** button and then, click a lighter blue swatch.

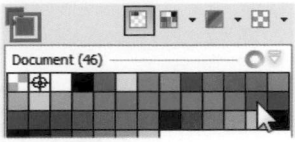

The flower petals are filled with the new colours.

3. Click to select the flower centre. Repeat step 2 to apply an orange outline and a yellow fill.

4. Click to select the flower stem. On the **Swatch** tab, click the arrow on the **Palettes** button and select **Standard RGB** from the drop-down list. Click the **Line** button and then, click a dark green swatch.

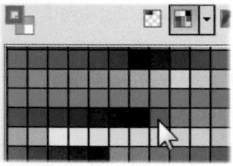

If you have problems when selecting objects which are lower down in the z-order, press the **Alt** key while clicking.

5. Finally, select the leaves. On the **Swatch** tab, apply a dark green line, and a lighter green fill. (If you can't find a colour that you like, try selecting a different palette.)

   Your flower is complete!

Any colours that are used in your document are added to the **Document Palette** so that they are easy to find and reuse!

Save now! Click **File > Save As...** and choose a new name for your file.

Next, we're going to look at copying formatting from one object to another. We're going to use another flower for this.

To copy line and colour formatting:

1. Create another copy of the original flower.

2. With the **Pointer Tool**, click to select the coloured leaves, and then on the Standard toolbar, click **Format Painter**.

3. Click on the black and white leaves of the copy. They update immediately.

4. Repeat this technique to colour the stem and centre of the flower.

The **Format Painter** applies the colour and line properties (including weight, type, opacity, etc.) to an object. It doesn't affect the size of shape. Try it for yourself on some of the other shapes in the file! For more information about the **Format Painter**, see DrawPlus Help.

To apply a solid fill and line colour (Colour tab):

1. With the **Pointer Tool**, click to select the black and white petals of the copy.

2. On the **Colour** tab the **HSL Colour Wheel** should be displayed. (If not, select it from the drop-down list.)

   - Click the **Line** button and then, click in the triangle to select a colour saturation. To change the Hue, drag the small black circle in the outer wheel to a new location.

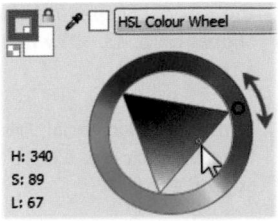

   - Click the **Fill** button and then, repeat the process above to select a lighter fill colour.

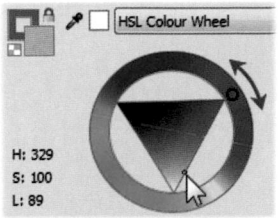

   Your second flower is complete!

Don't forget to save your work!

When choosing line colours for cartoons, instead of using black, try a darker version of your fill colour. We think you'll be pleased with the results!

We used a combination of these three fill techniques to complete our cartoon animals, created in the tutorial *Shapes II: Modifying Shapes* on p. 43. Why not give it a try yourself?

In the final fill tutorial, *Fills II: Gradient Fills* on p. 57, we'll look at gradient fills.

Brushes I: Using Brushes

The DrawPlus X5 **Brushes** tab includes a wide selection of pressure-sensitive, artistic brushes. Many of the brushes allow you to create natural media strokes created by 'real' paintbrushes, pens, pencils, and other media. They are even applied in a similar way to the real thing!

In this tutorial, we'll introduce you to this exciting collection of drawing tools and show you how to use the brushes in your drawings.

By the end of this tutorial you will be able to:

- Convert line to brush strokes.
- Draw with brush strokes.
- Edit brush lines.
- Change brush stroke attributes.

We'll demonstrate a couple of techniques and illustrate how you can create different effects by adjusting brush stroke style and attributes.

We're going to work with the bunny drawing that we create in the tutorial *Shapes II: Modifying Shapes* on p. 43. You can either create your own drawing or follow our tutorial exactly by working from our file.

Go to **http://go.serif.com/resources/DPX5** to download the following tutorial project file(s):

bunny.dpp

Let's begin...

- On the Standard toolbar, click **Open**.
- Locate **bunny.dpp** and click **Open**.

At the moment, the bunny looks like a cartoon drawn with QuickShapes as it has smooth vector outlines.

There are two ways that we can give it a hand-drawn look:

- Convert the existing lines to brush strokes using the **Line** tab.
- Use the original lines as a guide (on Layer 1), and trace over them with the *Paintbrush Tool* (on another layer).

Save now! Click **File > Save As...** and choose a new name for your file.

To convert lines to brush strokes:

1. With the **Pointer Tool**, click and drag to create a selection around the bunny. On release, the objects are selected.

2. On the **Line** tab, click the **Brush Stroke** button. The default brush stroke is applied. Change the **Cap** style to **Projecting Line Cap**.

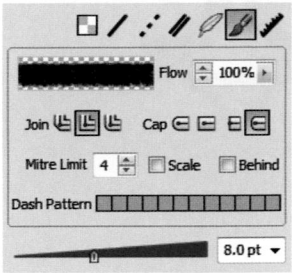

3. Drag the slider to increase the line width to **8** pt. (Or type **8** into the Width input box.)

4. On the **Brushes** tab, in the drop-down brush category list, click **Draw**.

5. Finally, click the **Graphic Soft Outline 03** brush. Immediately, the bunny takes on a hand-drawn effect!

Zoom at 40%

Zoom at 200%

The Paintbrush tool

The **Paintbrush Tool** allows you to draw or paint with natural looking lines. DrawPlus includes 'stroke' and 'spray' brushes, stored on the **Brushes** tab. Here, brushes are divided into categories depending on their appearance. We'll be focussing on the ones in the **Draw** category.

The **Paintbrush Tool** and the available brushes (and also the **Pencil Tool**) are pressure sensitive and will look very natural when used with either a pen and graphics tablet, or by using a combination of the mouse and **Pressure** tab (details are available in DrawPlus Help).

A pen and tablet works in a similar way to pencil and paper! With the pen, press and drag on the tablet to draw a line. Lift the pen to stop drawing. If you want a heavy, thick line, press hard on the tablet. For a thin, light line, use the pen lightly on the tablet. To select a line (or object, button etc.), hover the cursor over the line and then tap the pen on the tablet (this is the same as clicking with the left mouse button). You can also fine-tune any line using the **Pressure** tab. For the greatest control, don't forget to set up your tablet using the **Pressure Studio**. See DrawPlus Help for details.

We'll look at this process now by tracing our bunny onto a new layer to achieve the results similar to that displayed in the example below.

Zoom at 40%

Zoom at 200%

To make the bunny easier to trace, we first selected all of objects on Layer 1 and, on the **Colour** tab, we reduced the line **Opacity** to **30%**.

To draw with the Paintbrush Tool:

1. On the Standard toolbar, click **Open** and locate the original **bunny.dpp** file and click **Open**.

2. On **Layers** tab, click **Add Layer**. A new layer is added above Layer 1.

3. On the Hintline toolbar, use the Zoom buttons (or slider) to zoom into your drawing so that the bunny fills most of the workspace.

4. On the Drawing toolbar, click the **Paintbrush Tool**.

5. On the **Brushes** tab, in the drop-down brush category list, click **Draw**.

6. Click the **Graphic Soft Outline 03** brush. This is a 'stroke' bush, which is particularly good for drawing outlines.

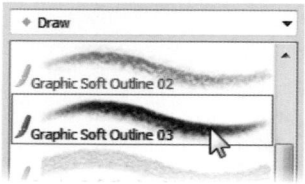

7. On the Brush context toolbar, set the **Width** to **8** pt, and the **Smoothness** to **40%**.

8. On the **Line** tab, set the **Cap** to **Projecting Line Cap** and the **Join** to **Rounded Join**.

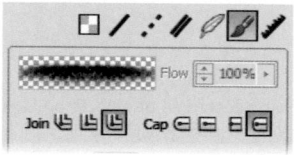

9. Use your pen and tablet (or mouse) to trace the first line by dragging on the page with the brush cursor.

10. Continue to trace around the outline of the bunny.

Save now! Click **File > Save As...** and choose a new name for your file.

Editing brush lines and attributes

If you make a mistake on any of you lines (as we have done), you can quickly edit the path of the line with the **Node Tool**. Let's look at this briefly now.

To edit a brush line:

1. With the brush cursor, click to select the brush stroke that you want to edit.

2. To temporarily switch to the **Node Tool**, click and hold the **Ctrl** key.

3. Click and drag on the line and the control handles until the line is correctly positioned.

Once you've completed your outline, you can also use the brushes to shade, paint or 'colour-in' your drawing. The 'spray' brushes are great for quickly filling in large blocks of colour, while the 'stroke' brushes tend to work best for cross-hatching and more traditional shading techniques.

For more details on creating and modifying lines, see the tutorial *Lines: Using the Pen Tool* on p. 75.

Don't forget to save your work!

To 'colour-in' with a brush:

1. On **Layers** tab, click **Add Layer**. A new layer is added above Layer 2. (We also hid Layer 1 by clicking .)

2. On the Hintline toolbar, use the Zoom buttons (or slider) to zoom into your drawing so that the bunny fills most of the workspace.

3. On the Drawing toolbar, click the **Paintbrush Tool**.

4. On the **Brushes** tab, in the drop-down brush category list, click **Draw**.

5. Click the **Chalk - Soft** brush. This is a 'spray' bush, which is particularly good for shading.

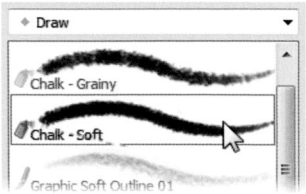

6. On the Brush context toolbar, set the **Width** to **6** pt and the **Smoothness** to around **20%**.

7. On the **Line** tab, set the **Cap** to **Projecting Line Cap** and the **Join** to **Rounded Join**.

8. Click and drag on the page, in the same way as you would shade in a drawing on paper, to shade in the pupil of the eye.

9. We can add some colour by simply changing the line colour on the **Colour** or **Swatch** tab. Here, we set the line to pink and coloured-in the nose.

10. Repeat the process, changing the brush type, colour and brush width until you have completely coloured-in your drawing. As we are working on a new layer, it doesn't matter if you go over the original lines, as we will fix that in a minute.

For more ways of colouring your drawings, see the tutorials *Fills I: Solid Fills* (p. 13) and *Fills II: Gradient Fills* (p. 57).

Don't forget to save your work!

To re-colour a brush stroke:

1. Click to select the line.

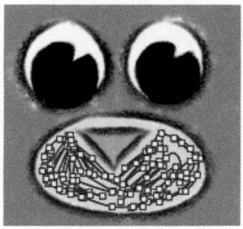

2. On the **Swatch** (or **Colour**) tab, click the **Line** button and then, select a new colour. The stroke is updated.

3. Finally, on the **Layers** tab, select layer 2 and click **Move Layer Up** to place it at the top of the stack. Your lines will now be on top of the coloured areas!

To finish our drawing, we applied a dark brown colour to our outline and created a background using a soft smudge brush for the sky, and a realistic grass brush from the brushes **Photo** category. (We also added some whiskers and a carrot!) For more on brushes, why not try the tutorial *Brushes II: Spray Brushes* on p. 65? Don't forget that you'll also find much more detail on editing the various settings in DrawPlus Help.

The Gallery

The DrawPlus **Gallery** tab provides you with a wealth of resources to help you create a multitude of different documents, charts, and drawings. The Gallery may not contain the exact object that you need, but it may contain something similar that you can use as a template to quickly create the object that you want. You can also add your own creations so that you can easily reuse them in future projects.

By the end of this tutorial you will be able to:

- Add Gallery objects to the page.
- Edit Gallery objects.
- Add your own creations to the Gallery.

Let's begin...

- In the Startup Wizard, choose **Start New Drawing**, select a page size of your choice and click **OK**.

To add a Gallery object to the page:

1. On the **Gallery** tab, in the category drop-down list, expand the **Clipart** category then click **Animals**.

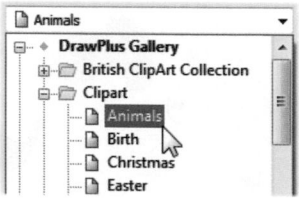

2. Using the **Pointer Tool**, drag the **Crab** from the **Gallery** tab to the page.

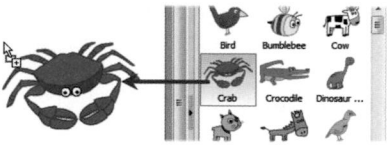

The object is placed on release.

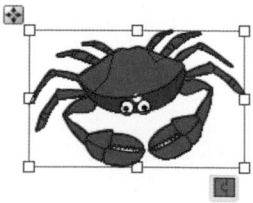

Most of the Gallery objects are **Grouped** objects. Any changes you apply to a group affect the whole group (including changes to fills and lines). To make any changes to individual elements, you'll first need to **Ungroup** the Gallery object.

Editing Galley objects

Any object in the Gallery can be modified to suit your own design. There are several ways of doing this and we can't hope to cover them all. However, as the basic steps are always the same, we'll give you a few ideas to get you started.

To create a silhouette from a Gallery object:

1. With the **Pointer Tool**, click the **Crab** to select it.

2. On the **Swatch** tab, click the **Line** button and then click a black swatch. A black outline is applied to all of the items within the group.

3. On the **Swatch** tab, click the **Fill** button and then click a black swatch. A black fill is applied to all of the items within the group.

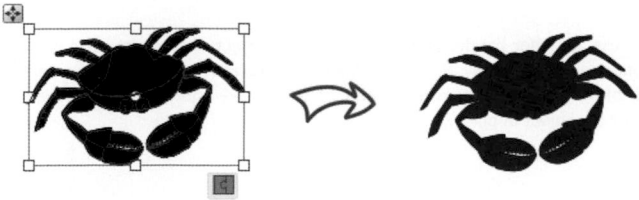

For more information on using the **Swatch** tab, see the tutorial *Fills I: Solid Fills* on p. 13.

To resize a Gallery object:

1. Using the **Pointer Tool**, drag another object from the **Gallery** tab to the page.

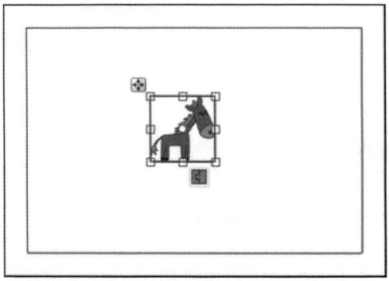

2. Make the image bigger by clicking and dragging on a corner handle.

If you use a corner handle to resize a grouped object, the aspect ratio is maintained automatically. If you press and hold **Ctrl** while resizing, the centre point of the object will remain 'locked' to the page—especially useful when resizing an object in place.

To change the colour of a Gallery object:

1. On the **Gallery** tab, in the category drop-down list, expand the **Clipart** category then click **Party**.

2. Using the **Pointer Tool**, drag the **Balloon** from the **Gallery** tab to the page.

3. Click **Ungroup**. On the **Layers** tab, you'll see that the balloon is made up of five objects.

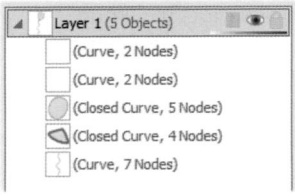

4. On the **Layers** tab, click the **Closed Curve, 5 Nodes** object. The main part of the balloon is selected.

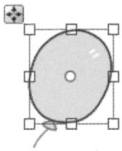

5. On the **Colour** (or **Swatch**) tab, apply a bright red **Fill** and a darker red **Line**.

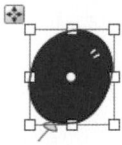

6. To format the end of the balloon, on the Standard toolbar, click **Format Painter**.

7. With the cursor, click the end of the balloon. The format is copied from the large shape to the small shape.

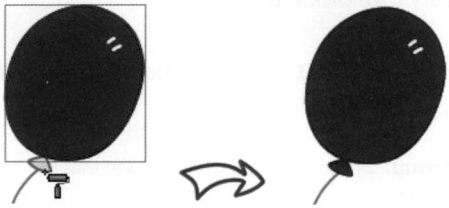

8. Finally, select all of the objects again and click **Group**.

Once you have ungrouped a Gallery object, you can also change the properties of individual elements. When you are happy with your changes, we always recommend that you Group the objects together again as this helps to structure a large drawing.

Here is an example we created using the balloon object. Some of these have been flipped or rotated to make each balloon slightly different.

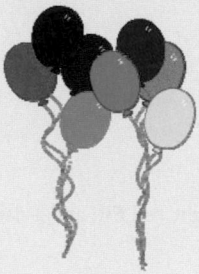

Storing your own content in the Gallery

One of the most useful things about the DrawPlus Gallery is the ability to add your own creations. This way, they are available for use in any future project. What's more, it's really easy to do!

To add an object to the Gallery:

1. On the **Gallery** tab, in the category drop-down list, expand the **My Designs** category.

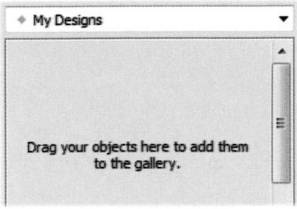

2. Using the **Pointer Tool**, drag your red balloon from the page to the **Gallery** tab.

3. In the dialog, type a name for your object and click **OK**. A copy of the object is added to the **Gallery** tab.

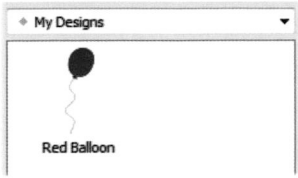

Gallery tips

You can add as many objects to the Gallery as you want. Here is an example of a few of the Gallery objects that we modified and then add to the Gallery:

If you know you'll be using the Gallery a lot, you should probably think about creating your own categories to organize your work.

To create a category:

1. Click the **Gallery Tab Menu** button.

2. Click **Add Category...**

3. Type a name for your category and click **OK**.

Now that you've seen how easy it is to place and edit Gallery objects, you can apply the same technique to any item in the DrawPlus Gallery. Take the time to explore the Gallery and you'll also find some useful examples for schoolwork and technical drawing. We'll leave you with a few more examples of images created using Gallery objects.

Example 1

Example chemistry diagram created from objects in **School > Sciences > Chemistry > Laboratory Equipment**.

The black objects are straight out of the Gallery, the red lines were drawn with the **Straight Line Tool** and the **Quick Ellipse**.

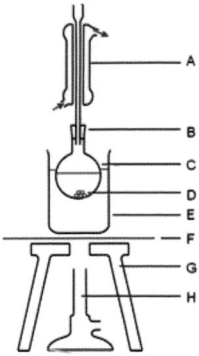

Example 2

Example electrical circuit created from objects in **School > Design & Technology > Electronics**.

The black objects are straight out of the Gallery, the red lines were drawn with the **Straight Line Tool**.

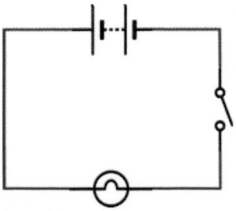

Example 3

Example flowcart created from objects in **Office > Flowcharts - Connecting > Designed**.

The objects are lined with the **Connector Tool**. For more information, see DrawPlus Help.

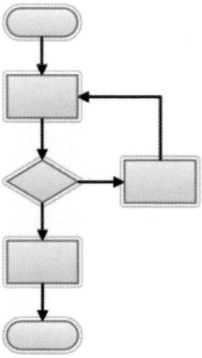

Shapes II: Modifying Shapes

In this tutorial we are going to draw several cartoons by using only basic QuickShapes! If you haven't done so already, you might find it easier to complete the tutorial *Shapes I: Drawing with QuickShapes* on p. 7 first.

By the end of this tutorial you will be able to:

- Create a variety of QuickShapes.
- Use **Convert to Curves** to create new shapes.
- Use the **Node** tool to transform shapes and lines.
- Copy shapes.

If you look at the opening example, you'll notice that the cartoons all start from a basic pear shape. To create this, we will modify a Quick Ellipse using **Convert to Curves** and the **Node Tool**.

Let's begin...

- In the Startup Wizard, choose **Start New Drawing**, select a page size of your choice and click **OK**.

Save now! Click **File > Save As...** and choose a new name for your file.

Converting an object to curves

If you want to dramatically modify your QuickShape, you'll need to 'convert it to curves'. This basically means that it stops being a QuickShape and instead becomes an object made up of a line with curved segments.

Although we are using a QuickShape in this tutorial, you can also convert text and other objects to curves in the same way. This is especially useful if you want to share artwork that uses an unusual font as it converts the text to shaped objects. This means that it will look the same, but will no longer be editable text, so the font isn't needed any more.

To convert a shape to curves:

1. On the Drawing toolbar, on the QuickShapes flyout, click the **Quick Ellipse** and drag on the page to create an ellipse.

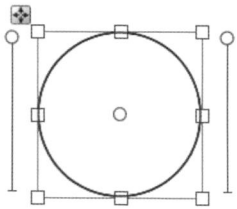

2. On the Drawing toolbar, click the **Node Tool**.

   With the shape selected, on the **Arrange** tab, click **Convert to Curves**. You'll see four 'nodes' appear on the ellipse's edge and the cursor changes to .

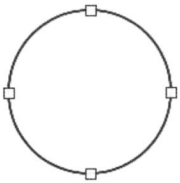

Save now! Click **File > Save As...** and choose a new name for your file.

Adjusting nodes

Converting a shape to curves allows you to edit it using the **Node Tool** and the **Curves context toolbar**. We'll do this next.

Lines and shapes consist of curve segments, nodes and control handles.

When you click on a node, the **node type** buttons become available for selection from the context toolbar. The behaviour of the control handles, and the curvature of the segments on either side of a node, depend on whether the node is sharp, smooth, symmetric, or smart. We can change the node type at any time.

(See 'Changing nodes and line segments' in the 'Editing lines and shapes' DrawPlus Help topic and the **How To** tab.)

To adjust a line with the Node Tool:

1. With the cursor, drag the topmost node upwards to create an egg shape.

2. Move the cursor over the line at the point where you want to add a node. When the cursor changes to click once to add a node.

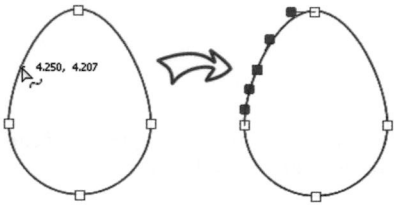

3. On the context toolbar, click **Sharp corner** to change the node type.

4. With the ⊳ cursor, drag the node handle upwards to change the shape of the line segment. The other segment doesn't change because we changed the node type to a sharp corner.

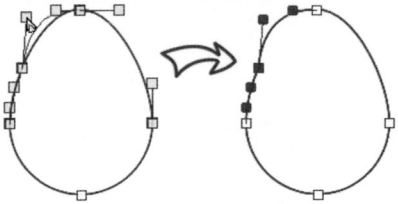

5. Drag the node in to decrease the width of the upper segment.

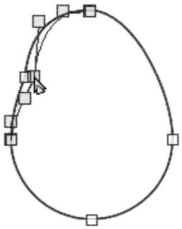

6. Repeat the add and adjust process for the other side of the shape so that it looks symmetrical.

7. To change the shape of the base slightly, select the node on the widest part, and with the ⊳ cursor, drag the handle downwards. Repeat for the opposite side.

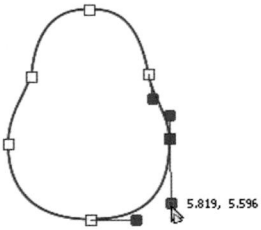

8. Finally to round the base off a little, select the bottom node and on the context toolbar, click **Symmetric corner**.

9. Drag the node handle inwards. Notice that both handles move in at the same time.

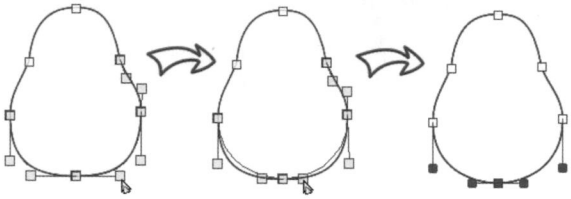

10. Your pear shape should now be complete and you've also learned how to edit lines with the node tool! This technique can be applied whenever you need to adjust a line.

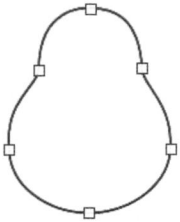

Now we have the basic pear shape, let's take a brief look at how we can use it.

Don't forget to save your work!

Example 1: Pear

To draw a pear:

1. Using the **Pointer Tool**, select the pear shape and copy it by holding the **Ctrl** key while dragging the shape. (Release the mouse button before the **Ctrl** key to complete the copy.)

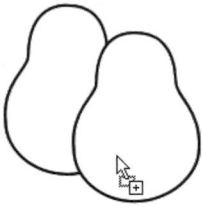

2. On the Drawing toolbar, on the QuickShapes flyout, click the **Quick Polygon** and drag on the page to create a polygon.

3. Drag the topmost node to the left to reduce the number of sides to 3.

4. Using the **Pointer Tool**, drag the side handle inwards to make the shape thinner.

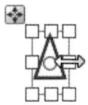

5. Hover next to a corner handle. When you see the ↻ cursor, drag the object to rotate it.

6. Finally, drag the 'stalk' into position using the ✥ Move button. Congratulations! You've drawn a pear!

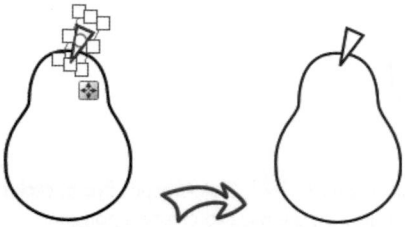

Hopefully you've now got the idea about how to copy, rotate, and manipulate the nodes of QuickShapes. All of the following examples use our pear shape plus some other QuickShapes. We'll point these out in the 'shapes used' section, but it's up to you to figure out how they go together!

Don't forget to save your work!

Example 2: Penguin

The body of the penguin uses a copy of the pear shape. The wings, eyes and feet are basic QuickShapes:

- The wings are made from a single **Quick Polygon** which we copied and flipped using **Flip Horizontal** on the **Arrange** tab (also available from the Standard toolbar).

- The eyes are created from two **Quick Ellipses**. The 'pupil' is created by adjusting the nodes on the ellipse to create the shine. The right eye is a copy of the left.

Shapes used:

- 'Pear' (black)
- Quick Ellipse (red)
- Quick Polygon (blue)

Save time and effort by copying elements that you have already created! You can always flip or rotate the copy if necessary.

Don't forget to save your work!

Example 3: Rabbit

With the exception of the whiskers (**Pen Tool**), the rabbit is also made out of three basic shapes. Again, where we had two elements that were basically the same, we saved time by copying and flipping the element using the **Arrange** tab.

Shapes used:

- 'Pear' (black)
- Quick Ellipse (red)
- Quick Polygon (blue)
  - and -
- Pen Tool (green lines)

You can re-arrange the **Z-order** of your objects using the tools— **Bring to Front**, **Forward One**, **Back One** and **Send to Back**— on the **Arrange** tab. See DrawPlus Help for more information.

Don't forget to save your work!

Example 4: Mouse

Our little mouse uses three basic shapes, but the tail shape was drawn with the **Pen Tool**. We made sure that we created a closed shape as this will enable us to fill the tail at a later date.

Shapes used:

- 'Pear' (black)
- Quick Ellipse (red)
  - and -
- Pen Tool (green lines)

Don't forget to save your work!

Example 5: Cat

Our cat uses similar shapes, but we squashed the 'pear' a little to make him a fat cat! We also used a new shape, the **Quick Shield**, for the ears, nose and mouth.

Shapes used:

- 'Pear' (black)
- Quick Ellipse (red)
- Quick Shield (purple)
  - and -
- Pen Tool (green lines)

Don't forget to save your work!

Example 6: Horses

The horses might look complicated, but they still only use basic QuickShapes. The head is made from a resized copy of the original pear shape that has been flipped using **Flip Vertical** on the **Arrange** tab. The mane and tail are created using short lines drawn with the **Pencil Tool**.

Shapes used:

- 'Pear' (black)
- Quick Ellipse (red)
- Quick Polygon (blue)
- Quick Rectangle (purple)
  - and -
- Pencil Tool (green lines)

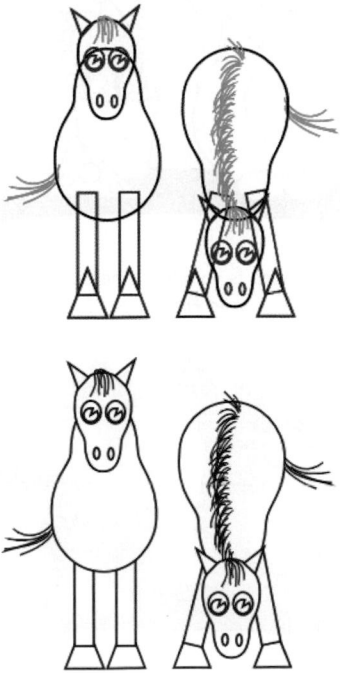

Don't forget to save your work!

Now you've created your cartoons, why not add a few more shapes to make a background. In the cat and mouse example, we've used our QuickShape flowers, a **Quick Cylinder** modified in the same way as the "pear" to create the flower pot, a **Quick Ellipse** for the mouse hole and a **Quick Polygon** for the cheese (of course, it's holey cheese so we used a few **Quick Ellipses** too!).

The next step is to add some colour! You'll find out how easy it is in the tutorial *Fills I: Solid Fills* on p. 13.

Fills II: Gradient Fills

In this tutorial, we are going to add gradient fills to some of the shapes created in the tutorials *Shapes I: Drawing with QuickShapes* and *Shapes II: Modifying Shapes* on p. 7 and p. 43, respectively.

By the end of this tutorial you will be able to:

- Apply gradient fills from the **Swatch** tab.
- Apply gradient fills with the **Fill Tool**.
- Edit gradient fill colours.
- Use the **Fill Tool** to edit gradient fill paths.
- Save a gradient fill for later use.

Go to **http://go.serif.com/resources/DPX5** to download the following tutorial project file(s):

quickshapes.dpp

Let's begin...

- On the Standard toolbar, click **Open**.
- Locate **QuickShapes.dpp** and click **Open**. Alternatively, if you have completed the previous tutorials, open the document containing the flower shapes.

Gradient fills

Gradient fills can quickly add a lot more depth to your drawings by creating subtle shading. Once you know how to apply them, they are very quick, easy and effective to use. Although this tutorial concentrates on fills, gradient can be applied to lines in exactly the same way!

The following example shows a few different gradient fills that would suit our QuickShape flowers.

Solid **Linear** **Radial** **3 Colour** **4 Colour**

There are several ways to apply gradient fills, let's look at those now.

Create a copy first!

For this tutorial, each new gradient is going to be applied to a copy of the blue flower we created in *Fills I: Solid Fills* on p. 13.

To apply a gradient fill (Swatch tab):

1. With the **Pointer Tool**, select the blue flower with the solid fill. Hold the **Ctrl** key and drag the selected objects to create a new copy.

2. On the new copy, click to select the petals.

3. On the **Swatch** tab, click arrow on the **Gradient Palettes** button and select **Three Colour** from the drop-down list. Click the **Fill** button and then, click a blue gradient swatch to apply the gradient.

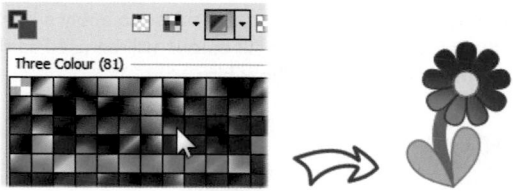

To apply a linear gradient fill (Fill Tool):

1. With the **Pointer Tool**, select the blue flower with the solid fill. Hold the **Ctrl** key and drag the selected objects to create a new copy.

2. On the new copy, click to select the petals.

3. On the Drawing toolbar, click the **Fill Tool**.

4. On the context toolbar, ensure that **Apply to Fill** is selected.

5. Drag from one side of the petals to the other to apply a linear gradient. By default, your current fill colour will be used as the start colour, and the end colour will be white.

You can also apply gradient fills to lines! On the context toolbar, ensure that **Apply to Line** is selected and then use the **Fill Tool** in exactly the same way as if you were applying the gradient to the object's fill.

Save now! Click **File > Save As...** and choose a new name for your file.

Editing gradient fills with the Fill Tool

You can edit a gradient fill at any time. Clicking a new gradient swatch on the **Swatch** tab will replace the current fill. To edit the current fill, you need to use the **Fill Tool**.

To change a fill type:

1. With the **Pointer Tool**, select the blue flower with the solid fill. Hold the **Ctrl** key and drag the selected objects to create a new copy.

2. On the new copy, click to select the petals.

3. On the Drawing toolbar, click the **Fill Tool**.

4. On the Context toolbar, change the **Fill Style** to **Radial**. The fill is updated.

To change key colours (Context toolbar method):

1. With the petals selected, click the **Fill Tool**.

2. On the Context toolbar, select a new colour from the **Fill Start** drop-down list (we chose white).

3. Select a new colour from the **Fill End** drop-down list (we chose red). The fill is updated.

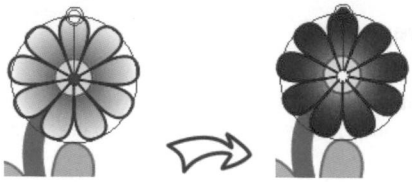

To change key colours (tab method):

1. With the petals selected, click the **Fill Tool**.

Depending on the type of fill applied (linear, radial, ellipse, etc.), a fill path is displayed as one or more lines, with nodes marking where the spectrum between each key colour begins and ends.

2. Select a node with the node cursor, and then on the **Swatch** (or **Colour**) tab, click a new colour.
   - or -

   Drag from a colour swatch on to any node to change the key colour of the node. The cursor displays when you are over a node. Note that the node doesn't need to be selected.

To add a key colour:

- Drag from a colour swatch on to a portion of the fill path where there is no node. The cursor changes to include a plus (+) sign.

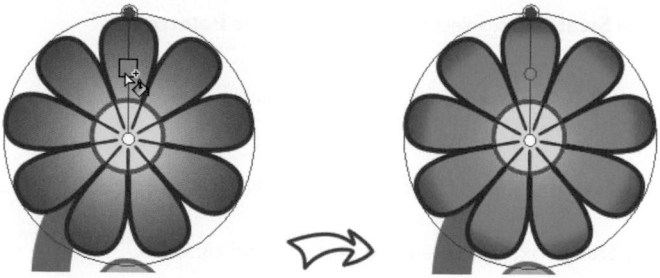

To delete a key colour:

- Select a colour node and press the **Delete** key.

To change the colour spread:

- Click and drag the fill path nodes.
  - or -
- Drag the start and end path nodes.
  - or -
- Click on a new location for the start node and drag out a new fill path.

Don't forget to save your work!

To save a gradient fill:

1. On the **Swatch** tab, select the **Document Palette**.

2. With the **Pointer Tool**, select the object containing the fill you want to save.

3. Right-click on the object and in the menu click **Add to Studio>Fill...**

4. In the dialog box, type a name for your fill and click **OK**.

   Your fill is added to the **Document Palette**.

That's it! You should now be able to apply and edit gradient fills to any object. All it takes is a little practice.

To conclude this set of tutorials, here's an image created from only QuickShapes, the **Grass** spray brush (see p. 65), and the fill techniques that you have just learned. Why not try creating it yourself? Have fun!

Brushes II: Spray Brushes

As we've seen in the tutorial *Brushes I: Using Brushes* on p. 21, the **Brushes** tab includes a wide selection of artistic brushes. Spray brushes in particular are great for filling in and shading large areas, just as an airbrush would be in the non-digital world. Many of the DrawPlus spray brushes create photo-realistic textures on the page.

In this tutorial, we'll focus on spray brushes to create an image similar to one found in the DrawPlus X5 Samples.

By the end of this tutorial you will be able to:

- Use layers for different brush strokes to add depth to an image.
- Copy an image from one file to another.
- Export a completed image to a new file.

Go to **http://go.serif.com/resources/DPX5** to download the following tutorial project file(s):

night.dpp

Let's begin...

- On the Standard toolbar, click **Open**.
- Locate the **night.dpp** file and click **Open**.

Using the spray brushes

In the following sections, we'll use a selection of spray brushes to add clouds and trees to our starting image.

Save now! Click **File > Save As...** and choose a new name for your file.

On the **Brushes** tab, the spray brushes are denoted with the icon. Spray brushes may be based on photo images or textures. Both can be recoloured.

Using layers to build up a drawing

To create our finished image, we're going to add various brush strokes to various layers within the document. We'll start by using a brush to add a few clouds.

To add the clouds:

1. On the **Layers** tab, click on the **Clouds 1** layer to make it the active layer.

2. On the Drawing toolbar, click the **Paintbrush Tool**.

3. On the **Brushes** tab, in the drop-down brush category list, click **Nature** and then, click the **Fog** brush.

4. On the **Swatch** tab, click the **Line** button and then, click a light grey swatch.

5. At the top of the workspace, on the Brush context toolbar, set the brush **Width** to **200** pt and the **Opacity** to **20%**.

6. Click and drag a zig-zag line down the page to paint a layer of cloud in the sky. The cloud appears behind the moon as it's on the layer below the **Moon** layer.

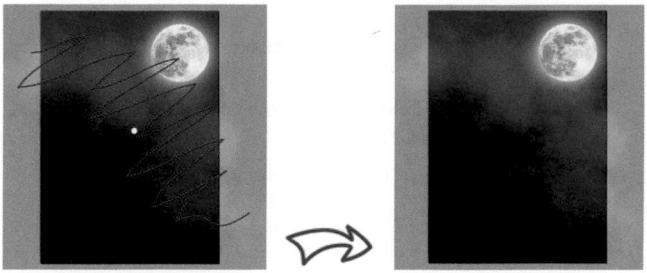

Next we'll add some cloud in front of the moon.

7. On the **Layers** tab, click on the **Clouds 2** layer to make it the active layer.

8. On the **Swatch** tab, set the line colour to the lightest grey swatch.

9. On the Brush context toolbar, set the brush **Width** to **124** pt and the **Opacity** to **100%**.

10. Click and drag across the page to paint some cloud across the moon.

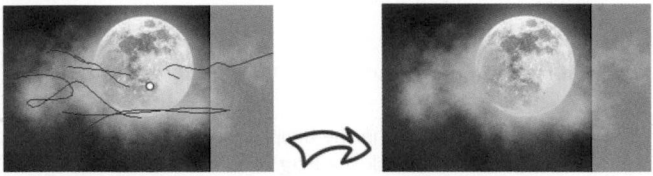

11. Continue building up the cloud until you've achieved the effect you want. Vary the opacity of different strokes can help make the cloud look more authentic.

Don't forget to save your work!

To add the trees:

1. On the **Layers** tab, click on the **Trees 1** layer.

2. On the **Brushes** tab, in the **Nature** category, click the **Trees** brush.

3. On the Brush context toolbar, set the brush **Width** to **200** pt and the **Opacity** to **100%**.

4. Click and drag a free-flowing line in the lower section of your page to create the treetops.

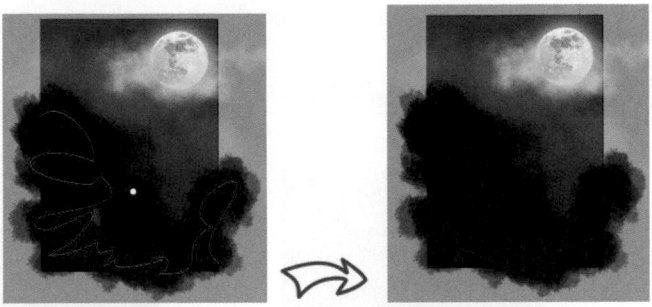

Next we'll add some foreground trees.

5. On the **Layers** tab, click on the **Trees 2** layer.

6. On the **Brushes** tab, in the **Nature** category, click the **Moss** brush.

7. On the Brush context toolbar, set the brush **Width** to **200** pt and the **Opacity** to **100%**.

8. Click and drag a free-flowing line in the lower section of your page to create the treetops.

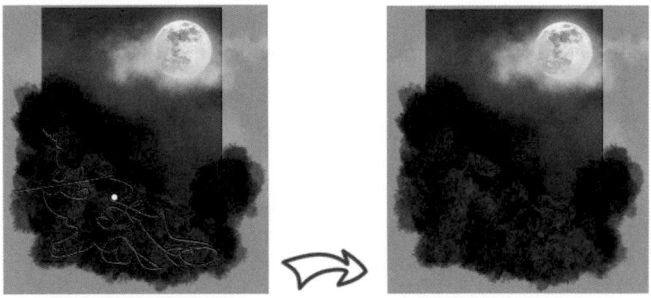

9. Finally, on the **Layers** tab, click on the **Trees 3** layer.

10. On the **Swatch** tab, set the line colour to a yellow swatch.

11. With the **Moss** brush, paint a smaller line over the lower-left of the tree section. The 'photo' spray brush colour is altered to have a yellow hue.

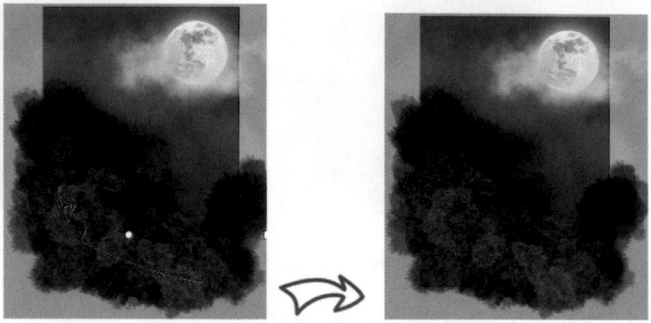

Spray brushes can be created with two types of images—a simple 8-bit black and white image and a full colour high resolution image. The ones created with an 8-bit black and white image can be fully re-coloured from the **Colour** or **Swatch** tabs. With the full colour or 'photo' spray brushes, when you select a new colour, only the hue will change and they will retain a lot of the original characteristics. Why not try creating your own brushes in the tutorial *Creating Brushes* on p. 91?

That's it! Your spray brush work is complete.

Don't forget to save your work!

Optional step: Adding the silhouette

To complete our night image, we added a couple of bat silhouettes. We've included the bat in the DrawPlus file, **silhouettes.dpp** for you to use.

silhouettes.dpp

To add the silhouette:

1. On the **Layers** tab, click on the **Silhouette** layer to make it the active layer.
2. On the **File** menu, click **Open**.
3. Browse to your **silhouettes.dpp** file and click **Open**.
4. Right-click the silhouette you want to use in your image and click **Copy**. Close the **silhouettes.dpp** file.
5. Back in the **night.dpp** file, right-click on the page and click **Paste**.
6. Drag the pasted silhouette into position, resizing it as required.

To create additional silhouettes, simply create copies. Don't forget that you can flip, rotate and resize the silhouettes.

Exporting your finished image

As you can see, we've extended passed the boundaries of the page. This doesn't matter as DrawPlus will tidy things up when we export the image.

To export an image to a new file:

1. On the **File** menu, click **Export > Export as Image...**

2. In the **Image Export** dialog:

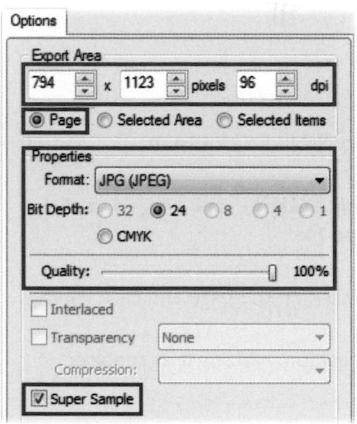

- The **Export Area** shows the dimensions of your current image in pixels at the displayed 96dpi (dots per inch). To change the printed resolution, increase or decrease the dpi.

- Ensure that the **Page** option is selected.

- Choose the file type from the **Format:** drop-down menu and set the output quality if applicable (as in our example).

- Select **Super Sample** (if available) to improve the look of lines and text.

- Click **Export**.

- To complete the export, browse to the folder in which you want to create the file, give it a file name and click **Save**.

The options available in the **Image Export** dialog are dependent on the export format that has been selected. For information about the different options, see DrawPlus Help.

If you've followed all of the steps in this tutorial, you should now have an image that resembles ours.

We hope you've enjoyed working with the spray brushes. Remember, the best way to find out what each brush does is to experiment freely. Have fun!

We look forward to seeing your spray brush creations on the www.drawplus.com website!

Lines: Using the Pen Tool

Being able to draw and edit lines is an essential technique to learn in DrawPlus. In this tutorial, we'll look at one of the most common ways to use the **Pen Tool** to digitize (trace over) an original drawing.

By the end of this tutorial you will be able to:

- Import an image file.
- Trace around an object using the **Pen** tool.
- Adjust curves using nodes and control handles.

While mastering the **Pen** and **Node Tools** won't necessarily be easy, they are amongst the most useful tools that DrawPlus has to offer and will open up endless possibilities for your artwork.

Let's begin...

- In the Startup Wizard, choose **Start New Drawing**, select a page size of your choice and click **OK**.

Scanning and importing your original drawing

It's not easy to create a digital drawing from scratch. Most of us are much more familiar with drawing on paper using traditional media. So, how do we get started? Many designers will create their drawing or artwork on paper first and then either scan it, or photograph it with a digital camera. Once the drawing is in a digital format, we can easily import it into DrawPlus so that we can start creating a masterpiece!

One thing to remember, you shouldn't think of this method of digitizing a drawing as 'cheating', instead think of it as a genuine technique that's used by artists all over the world!

So that you can follow the tutorial, we've provided an image of our funky skateboarding superhero, Kit. (You'll also find a sample included with DrawPlus X5 that shows Kit's character model sheet in all of its glory!)

Go to **http://go.serif.com/resources/DPX5** to download the following tutorial project file(s):

kit.png

The drawing that we are working on is quite complex and will take time to trace. You don't have to trace the entire image if you don't want to! Remember, you can use any image or only trace part of our drawing, such as the head. This tutorial is filled with helpful techniques that will help you become proficient with this powerful tool.

This method will work equally well to create a drawing from a photo.

To import the image:

1. On the Drawing toolbar, click **Insert Picture**.

2. In the **Insert Picture** dialog, locate the **kit.png** file, click to select it and then click **Open.**

3. Click and drag on the page to place the image so that it fills most of the page.

Optional: Sometimes you might find it easier to trace your image if you reduce its opacity as this can make it easier to see your newly created lines.
• With your image selected, on the **Colour** tab, click the **Fill** button.
• Drag the **Opacity slider** to the left until the image's opacity is reduced sufficiently.

4. On the **Layers** tab, click the small padlock button to lock the layer. This will prevent the drawing from accidentally being selected when we start the line work.

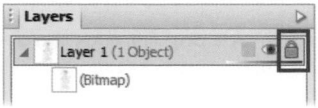

Save now! Click **File > Save As...** and choose a new name for your file.

Tracing the image

Now that we have our drawing on the page, the next thing to do is to trace an outline. Our drawing is already very 'clean', i.e., there aren't many extra sketch or construction lines. However, if you use your own drawing, it might be a very different story. When using the **Pen Tool**, we're aiming to create a nice, clean vector outline.

We'll create all of our lines on a new layer. This will keep things really simple and help us a lot if we decide to colour our image later on.

To create a new layer:

- On the Layers tab, click **Add Layer**. A new layer, Layer 2, is added above Layer 1 and is selected by default.

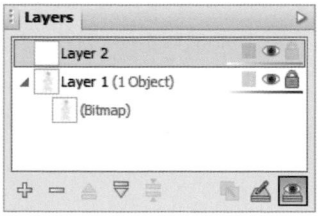

Now we're ready to start drawing. We're going to start with the head of our character so let's zoom in a little so that we can see what we're doing.

To zoom into an image:

- On the HintLine toolbar, click **Zoom In** or drag the Zoom slider to the right.

The Pen Tool

There are two main tools that you could use to trace an image:

- The **Pen Tool**—used for creating extremely accurate lines and shapes.

- The **Pencil Tool**—great for drawing freeform, pressure-sensitive lines and is particularly useful if you own (or use) a pressure sensitive drawing tablet.

In this tutorial we'll be concentrating on the **Pen Tool** as you will be able to transfer many of the skills, such as node editing, between the two types of line created.

Let's get started!

To create lines using Smart Segments:

1. On the Drawing toolbar, click the **Pen Tool** and on the context toolbar, ensure that **Smart segments** is selected.

> At the left of the context toolbar, notice that the **Pen Tool** has three creation modes:
>
> - **Smooth segments**
> - **Smart segments** (default)
> - **Line segments**
>
> These options let you create different types of curves and joins while you are drawing your line. See DrawPlus Help and the How To tab for detailed information.

2. On the **Colour** tab, ensure that the **Line** colour is set to black.

3. On the context toolbar (or on the **Line** tab), ensure that the line width is set to **1** pt.

4. Click where the first part of the hat starts near the goggles. Then, continue clicking at each point where there is a natural change in direction. The line should begin to update to match the curve as you place the nodes. If you make a mistake, don't worry as we can easily adjust the line later.

5. Once you have completed this first line, press the **Esc** key to tell DrawPlus that the line is complete.

At this point, we can either make adjustments to the line, or create another. Our line isn't exact, but it's pretty close, so we only need a small edit with the **Node Tool**. We can change to this temporarily by holding the **Ctrl** key.

To make quick adjustments to a line:

1. With the **Pen Tool** still selected, press and hold the **Ctrl** key. Notice that the cursor changes to a small arrow.

2. Move the cursor over the line, and when it changes to click and drag the line segment into position.

3. Repeat the process for any other segments as necessary.

Now that the first line is completed, we're ready to continue tracing around our character. This time we'll look at a slightly different way of using the **Pen Tool**. Instead of simply clicking to place a node, we can click and drag to shape the line as we place it.

To create lines using Smooth Segments:

1. On the Drawing toolbar, click the **Pen Tool** and on the context toolbar, ensure that **Smooth segments** is selected.

2. Click once to place your starting node at the point where the goggles and hat join and then click and drag to place the next node. As you drag, you'll notice that the shape of the line changes. As before, follow the natural change of direction of the line.

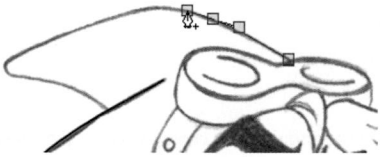

3. On **release**, the node is placed.

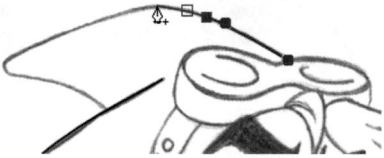

4. Repeat the click and drag process to complete the rest of the outline.

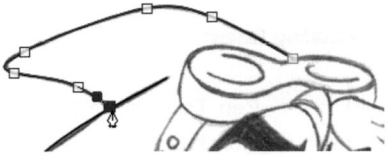

5. At the end of the line, press **Esc** (or you can also double-click when adding the last node if you find this easier).

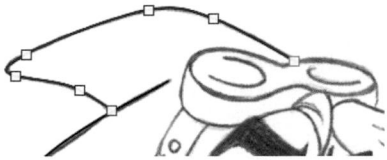

Remember, if you've made a mistake while placing a node, or if you just want to change the line, you can always modify it with the **Node Tool**. This is covered in detail in the tutorial *Shapes II: Modifying Shapes* on p. 43, the **How To** tab and in DrawPlus Help.

Don't forget to save your work!

Using Modifiers

Modifiers are keys that temporarily change the action of a tool while they are being pressed. DrawPlus uses lots of these modifiers and they provide quick shortcuts to do certain things.

The **Pen Tool** has some really useful modifier keys that change the type of node that is placed when you click. This allows you to more accurately place a line as it is created and hopefully reduces the amount of editing that you have to do later on using the **Node Tool**.

One really useful modifier is the **Alt** key. This adds a sharp node to the line so that you can create corners. Let's look at this now.

To use modifiers when drawing lines:

1. On the Drawing toolbar, click the **Pen Tool** and on the context toolbar, ensure that **Smooth segments** is selected.

2. Click on the sharp 'point' where the hair meets the goggles and then click and drag to create the first curved segment.

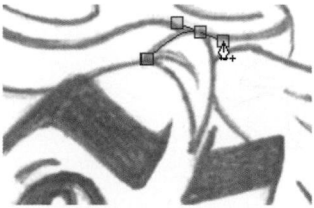

3. Next, click and drag on the point of the hair to create the next curved segment **but do not release the mouse button** yet. Once the curve is correct, press and hold the **Alt** key.

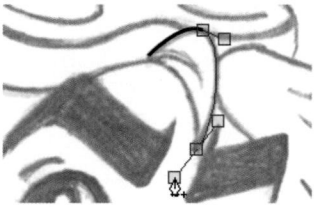

4. Still holding down the left-mouse button and **Alt**, position the control handle in the direction of your next curve segment, approximately where the next node will be, and **release** the **mouse** button. Finally, release the **Alt** key.

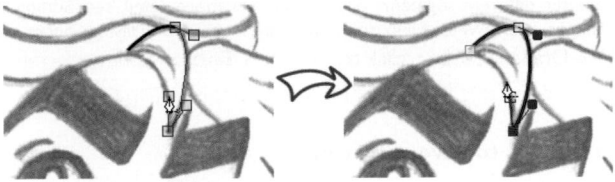

5. Click and drag to place the next node.

6. Finally, place the pointer over the green start node and click once the cursor changes to to close the line as a shape.

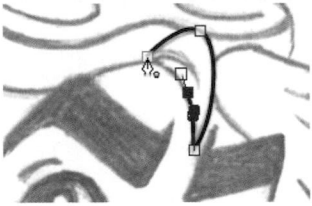

7. Your finished shape should not require any further editing and you can continue to trace the other parts of the drawing.

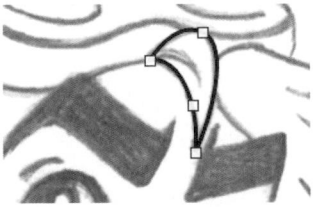

Even if you draw your lines with the help of modifier keys, there will be times when you need to have more control over editing your lines.

The **Node Tool** will give you the greatest control when you need to reshape the different segments of your line. For more detail, see 'Editing lines and shapes' in DrawPlus Help or the tutorial *Shapes II: Modifying Shapes* on p. 43.

Don't forget to save your work!

The finishing touch

Once you've finished tracing your image, on the **Layers** tab, click to hide **Layer 1** and the original drawing. You should end up with a neat line drawing consisting of even lines.

We can make this drawing look even better by varying the width of the lines to create a much more hand-drawn look. The best thing is that it will only take a minute!

To apply a pressure profile:

1. On the **Layers** tab, ensure that **Layer 2** is selected.

2. Using the **Pointer Tool**, drag a selection marquee over your entire drawing to select all of the lines.

3. On the **Line** tab, increase the line width to approximately **2.5** pt.

4. At the lower-right of the workspace, click on the **Pressure** tab heading to expand the tab.

5. In the pressure profile drop-down list, select the 7th profile.

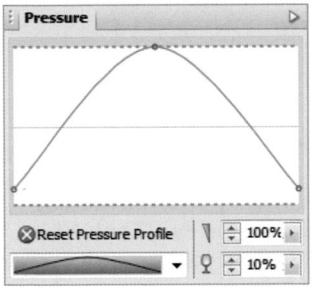

6. The lines on your drawing are updated!

Don't forget to save your work!

Congratulations on completing your drawing! By now you will have mastered the technique of drawing lines using the **Pen Tool**. A line drawing can be extremely dramatic by itself, but you may wish to consider enhancing your drawing with a splash of colour.

Adding colour

To complete your drawing, you may want to add colour. As the drawing is made up of mainly separate lines, you won't be able to do this by simply applying a fill.

Instead, we created a new layer and placed it below the layer containing the lines.

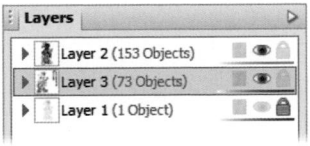

Using the **Pen Tool**, we created a new 'closed' shape for each different area of colour, removed the line and applied the appropriate fill (see *Fills I: Solid Fills* on p. 13). As the lines are on a different, higher layer, they always stay on top.

We've provided the completed file, **kit_complete.dpp** for you to have a look at.

Go to **http://go.serif.com/resources/DPX5** to download the following tutorial project file(s):

kit_complete.dpp

Creating Brushes

DrawPlus includes a wide selection of pressure-sensitive brushes as explored in the tutorials *Brushes I: Using Brushes* and *Brushes II: Spray Brushes* on p. 21 and p. 65, respectively. However, if you can't find the perfect brush for your project, you can also create your own!

By the end of this tutorial you will be able to:

- Create a new brush category.
- Create a non-repeating (stretching) stroke brush.
- Create a simple, repeating stroke brush.
- Create a spray brush.
- Copy and edit an existing brush.
- Sharing brushes.

Brush categories

DrawPlus includes 'stroke' and 'spray' brushes, stored on the **Brushes** tab. Here, brushes are divided into categories depending on their appearance.

To create a brush category:

1. On the **Brushes** tab, in the upper category drop-down list box, select **Global**.

2. Right-click on the category list box and click **Add...**

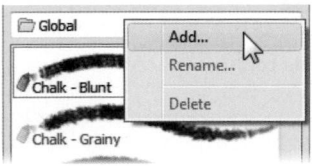

If you right-click on an existing category, your custom category will be added as a 'subcategory' of the selected category.

3. In the dialog, type a name for your category, e.g., My Brushes, and click **OK**.

4. The category displays in the tab's drop-down list.

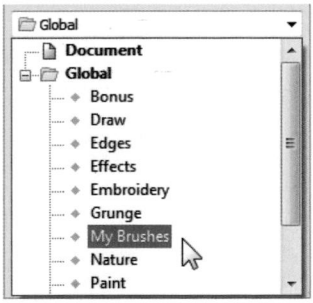

To rename a category:

- Right-click a category and choose **Rename**.

To delete a category:

- Right-click a category and choose **Delete**.

⚠ Do you really want to delete? Deleting categories and brushes will permanently remove them from the DrawPlus environment.

Brush textures

Before you start creating your brush, you need to choose the brush texture (design). A brush texture is simply a vector or bitmap file which is loaded for the brush type. There are several points to bear in mind:

- **File type and bit depth**
  - Any supported file format can be used, although we recommend using a 24 or 32 bit depth PNG with transparency for colour brushes.
  - An 8 bit depth greyscale (no transparency) PNG is recommended for black and white brushes.
  - If you aren't using an image with a transparent background, then your texture background should be pure white (RGB 255, 255, 255) as DrawPlus will create the transparency from this.
- **Shape/orientation**
  - **Stroke brushes**—For best results, the brush texture should be rectangular in shape with landscape orientation.

  - **Spray brushes**—The design can be of any shape and any orientation, ideally contained within a square boundary.

  - Crop as close as possible to the image so that there is very little or no white space around it.

- **Resolution**

  - **Stroke brushes**—This depends on the texture and repeat type, around 1500 pixels wide and 500 pixels high is good for most textures.

  - **Spray brushes**—For best results, the resolution should be 512 pixels wide by 512 pixels high.

Creating stroke brushes

Stroke brushes have two main types of body repeat method–**Stretching** and **Repeating**.

The following illustrations show how changing this setting affects the appearance of a brush stroke.

- **Stretching:** The 'body' of the brush is stretched along the length of the stroke.

- **Repeating:** A portion of the brush body is repeated over the length of the stroke.

  The number of times the portion is repeated is configurable and can range between one (**Simple**) and ten.

Now that you understand the basic principles, let's put them into practice. In the following section, we'll show you how to create:

- **a stretching bitmap photo brush**.

- **a simple one-part repeating bitmap texture brush**.

Stretching bitmap stroke brush

Assume now that we want to create a stroke brush based on an image of a pencil.

Go to **http://go.serif.com/resources/DPX5** to download the following tutorial project file(s):

pencil.png

You can create your brush textures from an exported drawing in DrawPlus as we have done for the pencil, or from a photo. Use Cutout Studio to remove the background and then export the image as a **24 or 32 bit depth PNG with transparency**. If you are creating a black and white brush, export the image as an **8 bit depth PNG without transparency**.

Let's begin...

- In the Startup Wizard, choose **Start New Drawing**, select a page size of your choice and click **OK**.

To create a stretching bitmap stroke brush:

1. Open the **Brushes** tab, in the category drop-down list, select the **My Brushes** category we created earlier on p. 92.

2. Right-click anywhere in the brushes list and click **Add Stroke...**.

3. In the **Stoke Brush Edit** dialog, click **Browse for a different texture**. In the **Open** dialog, browse to the **pencil.png** (32 bit depth with transparency) file and click **Open**.

4. The **Brush Name** box is populated with the name of your texture file. (You can change it if desired.)

5. In the **Category** drop-down list, select the category in which you want to save the brush, e.g., My Brushes.

6. In the **Body repeat method** drop-down list, select **None - (Stretch)**.

7. In the image preview window, note the vertical blue lines on either side of the image.

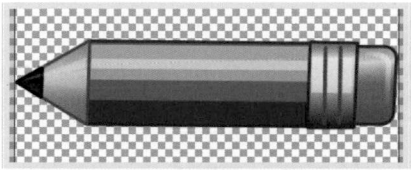

Click and drag these lines to define the **Head** and **Tail** (the sections you want to protect), and the **Body** (the section you want to stretch).

Note the updated values in the **Head**, **Body**, and **Tail** boxes.

8. Click **OK**.

9. Over on the **Brushes** tab, your new brush displays in the category you specified.

10. Make a few brush strokes to see what effects you can create... Why not try changing the line colour to see what happens?

One-part repeating bitmap texture brush

Let's now create a new stroke brush based on a repeating pattern. We are going to show you two examples, a paw print brush and a tyre tread.

Go to **http://go.serif.com/resources/DPX5** to download the following tutorial project file(s):

paw.png; tread.png

Example 1

The paw image is an easy image to create a repeating brush from as it has a good repeating pattern with plenty of 'white' space in between the patterns. This makes it easy to create seamless joins.

To create a bitmap texture brush:

1. Open the **Brushes** tab, in the category drop-down list, select the **My Brushes** category we created earlier on p. 92.

2. Right-click anywhere in the brushes list and click **Add Stroke...**.

3. In the **Brush Edit** dialog, click **Browse for a different texture.** In the **Open** dialog, browse to the **paw.png** (8 bit depth no transparency) file and click **Open**.

4. The **Brush Name** box is populated with the name of your texture file. (You can change it if desired.)

5. In the **Category** drop-down list, select the category in which you want to save the brush, e.g., My Brushes.

6. In the **Body repeat method** drop-down list, select **Simple**.

7. In the image preview window, note the vertical blue lines on either side of the image.

Click and drag these lines to define the **Head** and **Tail** (the sections you want to protect), and the **Body** (the section you want to repeat).

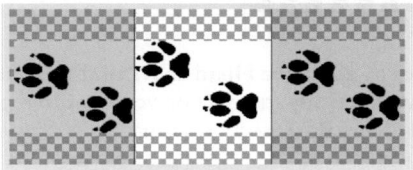

8. Click **OK**.

9. On the **Brushes** tab, your new brush displays in the category list you specified. Make a few strokes to try it out...

Example 2

All simple repeating brushes are created in this way. The trick is to ensure that your repeating section joins are seamless. To complete this section, we'll show you another simple repeating brush to give you an idea of how to create seamless joins on a more complex pattern.

- Repeat steps 1-7 to create your **tread.png** (8 bit depth no transparency) texture brush.

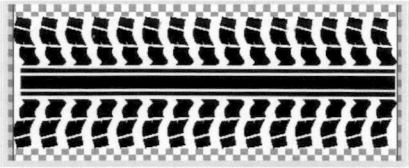

Click and drag these lines to define the **Head** and **Tail** (the sections you want to protect), and the **Body** (the section you want to repeat). Notice how we've lined up the **Body** section so that it will create a seamless repeat. (On some images, this may be a case of trial and error!)

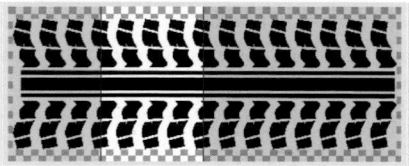

- Click **OK**.

- On the **Brushes** tab, your new brush displays in the category list you specified. Make a few strokes to try it out...

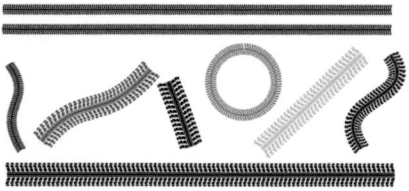

Creating spray brushes

Like stroke brushes, spray brushes can be based on any image type. The difference lies in the way they are created. Before you start creating your brush, you need to choose the texture (design) on which to base it. (See the *Brush textures* on p. 93 section for image guidelines.)

Let's now create a new spray brush based on a several images.

Go to **http://go.serif.com/resources/DPX5** to download the following tutorial project file(s):

bat1.png; **bat2.png**; **bat3.png**; **bat4.png**; **bat5.png**

To create a spray brush:

1. Open the **Brushes** tab, in the category drop-down list, select the *My Brushes* category we created earlier on p. 92.

2. Right-click anywhere in the brushes list and click **Add Spray...**

3. In the **Spray Brush Edit** dialog, click the **Click to add a spray nozzle...** button. In the **Open** dialog, browse to the file you want to use (**bat1.png**) for your new brush. Double-click the file, or select it and click **Open**.

   The **Brush Name** box is populated with the name of your texture file. (You can change it if desired.)

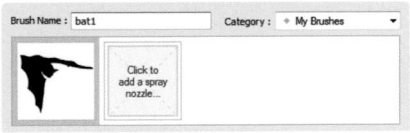

4. In the **Category** drop-down list, select the category in which you want to save the brush, e.g., My Brushes.

5. (Optional) Repeat step 3 to add additional nozzles (**Bat2.png**, **Bat3.png**, **Bat4.png** and **Bat5.png**).

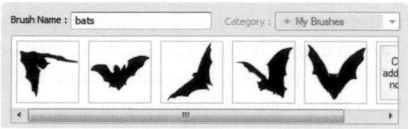

6. Adjust the settings described below to achieve the desired effect for your brush.

   - **Texture Selection Controller** (multiple nozzles only): This setting changes the way in which the various nozzle textures are applied to the page.

     For example, select **Random** to randomly mix up the order of nozzle textures; select **Pressure** to change nozzle texture according to the pressure applied with the brush (via pen and tablet or the **Pressure** tab).

   - **Position / Size Dynamics** settings: These settings change the positioning of the nozzle(s) as the brush is 'sprayed' on the page. (To create our bat brush, you'll need to increase the **Spacing** value to around 105%.) For detailed information on the settings, see DrawPlus Help.

   - **Rotation Dynamics** settings: These settings change the rotation of the nozzle(s) as the brush is sprayed on the page.

7. When you are happy with your brush design, click **OK** to save it to the **Brushes** tab.

8. Test out your new brush, varying the width of your strokes.

We also created a similar brush using full colour leaf images.

Go to **http://go.serif.com/resources/DPX5** to download the following tutorial project file(s):

leaf1.png ; **leaf2.png** ; **leaf3.png**

Remember, you can use as many overlapping lines as you need to when building up a texture!

Copying and editing brushes

At some point you'll want to make changes to an existing brush, or to a brush you've created yourself.

You can customize the predefined DrawPlus brushes. However, any changes you make will overwrite the existing brush presets so we suggest that you copy the brush to your own category before editing it (see *Brush categories* on p. 92).

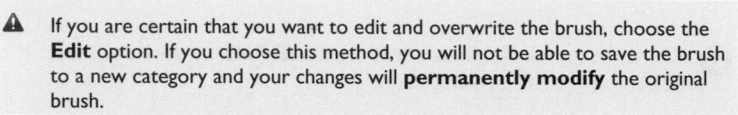

If you are certain that you want to edit and overwrite the brush, choose the **Edit** option. If you choose this method, you will not be able to save the brush to a new category and your changes will **permanently modify** the original brush.

To copy and edit a brush:

1. On the **Brushes** tab, right-click the brush you want to edit and click **Copy**.

2. In the **Brush Edit** dialog, you can:

   - Rename the brush. (Note that DrawPlus gives it the default name "Copy of ...")

   - Save the brush in a different category.

   - Change the repeat areas and the body repeat method (stroke brushes).

   - Browse for a different brush texture or nozzle (spray brushes).

   - Adjust texture selection controller, position dynamics, and rotation dynamics settings (spray brushes).

3. Make the desired changes and then click **OK** to save your edited brush.

> You can customize brush strokes directly using the Brush context toolbar—click the **Brush** option to open the **Stroke/Spray Brush Edit** dialogs. Any changes you make in this way will only affect the selected brush stroke and will not modify the brush stored in the gallery.

Sharing brushes

Once you've created a really nice set of custom brushes, you might want to share them with other DrawPlus users. As it happens, any brush that you have used in a document is saved with the .dpp project file.

To share brushes:

1. Begin a new document.

2. On the Drawing toolbar, click the **Paintbrush Tool**.

3. On the **Brushes** tab, select the brush that you want to share.

4. On the page, create a line.

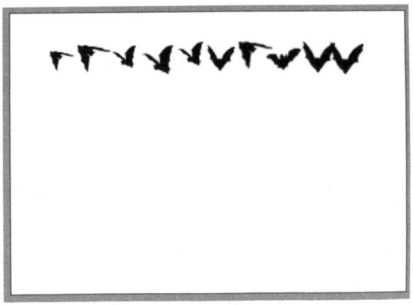

The brush appears in the **Document** category in the **Brushes** tab.

5. Repeat steps 3 and 4 for each brush that you want to share.

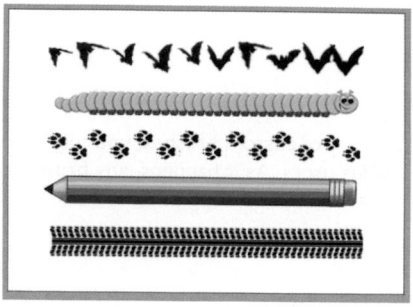

The **Document** category is updated for each new brush that is used.

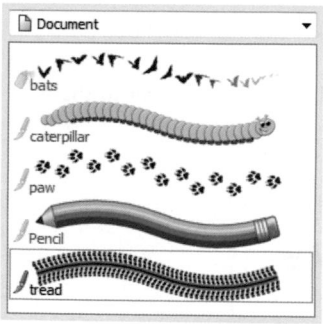

6. When you've completed your brush lines, click **File > Save As...** and choose a new name for your file, e.g., brushes.dpp

7. (Optional) Send the brushes.dpp file to your friend who can then add the brushes to their copy of DrawPlus by following the steps in the copying and editing brushes section on p. 104.

We've covered a lot of material in this tutorial—you've learned how to create a variety of different brushes, and how to copy and edit existing brushes.

We've introduced you to the basic procedures, but encourage you to get creative and try creating your own set of custom brushes.

And just in case you want to have a go at creating our cheerful caterpillar brush, we've provided the file for you!

Go to **http://go.serif.com/resources/DPX5** to download the following tutorial project file(s):

caterpillar.png

Text

DrawPlus offers three types of text to use in your projects, frame text, shape text, and artistic text.

You can use the same methods to perform operations such as selecting, editing, and formatting all types of text. For detailed information, see DrawPlus Help.

By the end of this tutorial you will be able to:

- Work with artistic, frame, and shape text.
- Create, edit, and format all types of text.
- Create text-on-a-path.
- Change the shape and fill of text frames.

In this tutorial, we'll add some text to a greetings card. You can either create a card from scratch using one of the folded publications templates (available from the **Start New Drawing** option on the Startup Wizard), or you can work with the card that we have already partially designed.

Go to **http://go.serif.com/resources/DPX5** to download the following tutorial project file(s):

card.dpp

Let's begin...

- On the Standard toolbar, click **Open**.
- Locate the **card.dpp** file and click **Open**.

The card opens with Page 1 displayed in the workspace.

Save now! Click **File > Save As...** and choose a new name for your file.

Artistic text

Let's start by adding some artistic text!

To create artistic text:

1. On the Drawing toolbar, click the **Artistic Text Tool**.
2. Click on the page to create an insertion point.

3. On the Text context toolbar, in the **Font** drop-down list, select **Apple Boy BTN** and set the size to **72** pt.

4. On the **Swatch** tab, select the **Fill** button and click a black swatch.

5. Type your greeting.

Next, we'll use the properties of artistic text to make it a little more exciting!

To resize and rotate artistic text:

1. With the **Pointer Tool**, click on the top-centre handle of the text box and drag upwards. Notice that this stretches the text.

2. Next, click right-centre handle of the text box and drag inwards. Notice that this squashes the text.

3. To rotate the text, hover next to a corner handle. When you see the ↻ cursor, click and drag to rotate the object.

4. Finally, click and drag the ✥ **Move** button to position the text.

Why not add some colour to your text? With the text box selected, go to the **Swatch** tab. Click the **Fill** button and then expand the **Gradient Fills** flyout. Then select a category and click one of the swatches to apply a gradient fill.

For more on using fills, make sure you visit the tutorials *Fills I: Solid Fills* and *Fills II: Gradient Fills* on p. 13 and p. 57, respectively.

Now that we've completed the front of our card, let's move on to the back. Here, we'll show you how to fit text to a curve. In the **Pages** tab, click to select page 4.

Don't forget to save your work!

Now let's create a new artistic text object...

To create artistic text (alternative method):

1. On the Drawing toolbar, click the **Artistic Text Tool**.

2. Click and drag on the page to set the font size to approximately **25** pt.

3. Type a card slogan (we used our website address).

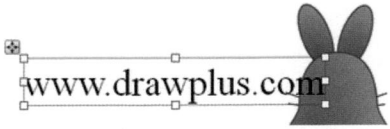

If you're not happy with the way the default font looks, you can easily change it. We'll do this next.

This method of formatting applies to all types of text.

To select and format existing text:

1. On the Drawing toolbar, click the A **Artistic Text Tool**.

2. Click inside the text box next to the first letter, and then drag to highlight all of the text. (You can also press **Ctrl** + **A** or triple click.) The selected text is highlighted blue.

3. On the Text context toolbar, in the **Font** drop-down list, select **Apple Boy BTN**.

4. On the **Swatch** tab, select the **Fill** button and click a green swatch. The text formatting is updated.

Don't forget to save your work!

Putting text on a path

Next, we'll fit our text to a curved path.

To put text on a path:

1. With the text object still selected, on the Text context toolbar, expand the **Preset Text Paths** flyout and click to apply the **Curved Text - Top Circle** preset.

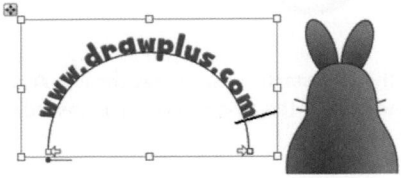

2. To adjust the path, hold the **Ctrl** key, and with the **Node Tool**, click the green start node and drag upwards.

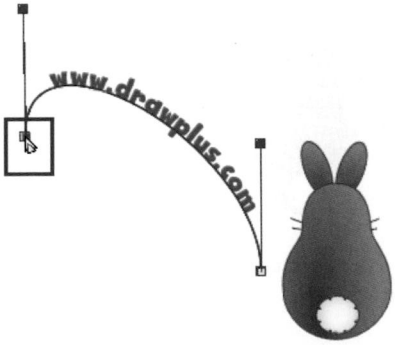

3. (Optional) To adjust the slope of the path, hold the **Ctrl** key, and with the **Node Tool**, drag the curve handle.

4. Finally, to change where the text starts, ensure that the A **Artistic Text Tool** is selected and click in the text to create an insertion point.

5. Drag the Start point arrow to the right to push the text towards the end of the curve.

6. Finally, to place the text beneath the curve line, drag the alignment node to the bottom of the bar.

7. That's it, your curved text is complete! If you've followed the steps exactly, the text should resemble our illustration.

You can also fit text to any curve, shape, or line that is drawn on the page. For more information, see 'Fitting text to a path' in DrawPlus Help.

Don't forget to save your work!

Adding text to shapes

Now let's make the inside of our card a little more interesting. In the **Pages** tab, click to select pages 2,3. On the inside pages of our card, we have a sunflower created from a Quick Petal and a Quick Ellipse.

Let's add our greeting to the inside of the flower (i.e. the Quick Ellipse).

To create shape text:

1. On the Drawing toolbar, click the A **Artistic Text Tool** and then click on the **Quick Ellipse**. An insertion point begins to flash in the centre of the shape.

2. On the **Swatch** tab, click the **Fill** button, and click the white swatch.

3. On the Text context toolbar, select the **Apple Boy BTN** font and set the font size to **36** pt. (You might need to adjust this to suit your message.)

4. Type the greeting you used on the front of the card.

Congratulations! You've just created shape text!

Don't forget to save your work!

Using text frames

We'll finish the card by creating a text frame.

To create a text frame:

1. On the Drawing toolbar, on the A Text Frames flyout, click the **Frame Text Tool**.

2. In the upper-left corner of the card, click and drag to create a small text frame.

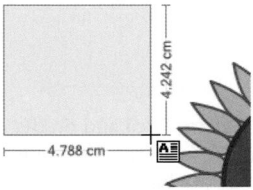

3. On the Text context toolbar, select the **Apple Boy BTN** font and set the size to **24** pt.

4. On the **Swatch** tab, click the **Fill** button, and click the black swatch.

5. Type 'To... '.

You have created a basic text frame. However, we don't have to stick with a basic rectangle. Let's get creative!

(Optional) To adjust the shape, line, and fill of a text frame:

1. With the **Pointer Tool** click to select the text frame.

2. On the **Line** tab, increase the line width to around **2** pt.

3. On the **Swatch** tab, apply a light fill and a black line.

4. On the Drawing toolbar, click the **Node Tool** and on the Context toolbar, choose **Quick Thought** from the Shaped frame drop-down menu. Adjust the direction of the bubbles by dragging the bottom node left or right.

5. Finally, with the **Pointer Tool**, resize the frame so that it fits all of your text. Notice that, unlike before, when you resize the frame, the text properties do not change as this is Frame Text.

6. Repeat steps 2-5 to create a "From" text frame. Why not try a different shape and line style?

Although a shaped text frame and shape text can look similar on the page, they are treated differently by DrawPlus. If you look at the **Layers** tab, text frames and artistic text always appear as text. However, shape text only appears as its containing shape. This is because text frames have very different behaviour. To find out more about adjusting text flow and linking text frames, see DrawPlus Help.

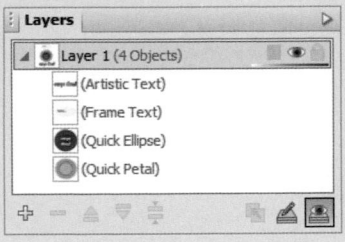

Don't forget to save your work!

That's it, your card is complete! You now know how to edit and format text, create text-on-a-path, and create new artistic, shape, and frame text objects.

The skills you have acquired should be sufficient for most of your DrawPlus projects!

Wax Seal

In this tutorial, we'll show you how to create a 'wax seal' effect. You'll use some basic QuickShapes and the **Freeform Paint Tool**, then apply filter effects to add depth and dimension to your shapes.

Once you've created your basic wax seal, you can get creative and adapt it for a multitude of purposes.

By the end of this tutorial you will be able to:

- Create new shapes using constrained QuickShapes and the **Freeform Paint Tool**.
- Use the **Colour** and **Line** tabs to apply properties to a shape.
- Use the **Filter Effects** dialog to apply bevel and emboss effects.
- Add Artistic text to your design.

Let's begin...

- In the Startup Wizard, choose **Start New Drawing**, select a page size of your choice and click **OK**.

Creating a new shape

We're going to use the **Freeform Paint Tool** to create an entirely new shape based on a simple QuickShape.

To create the basic shape:

1. On the Drawing toolbar, on the QuickShapes flyout, click the **Quick Ellipse**, then hold down the **Shift** key (to constrain the dimensions) and draw a circle about **10** cm in diameter.

   Let's now add a red fill to our circle.

2. On the **Colour** tab, click the **Fill** button, then, click a point in the red section of the colour wheel.

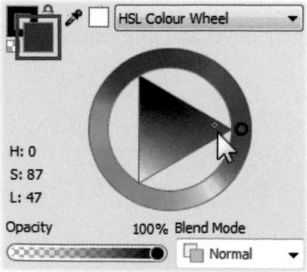

3. On the **Line** tab, remove the outline from your shape by clicking **No Line**.

4. On the Drawing toolbar, click the **Freeform Paint Tool** and on the context toolbar, select the **Round Nib** and increase the width to **30** pt.

5. Ensure that your circle is selected and click and drag at various points around your circle to create an uneven border.

On release, your shape is updated.

6. Vary the width of the nib on the context toolbar as you click and drag to add a few different size circular shapes to the border.

You can vary the nib width, and the click and drag process as much as you want to achieve the desired effect. Don't worry if your shape doesn't look exactly like our illustration—no two wax 'blobs' are alike!

Save now! Click **File > Save As...** and choose a new name for your file.

Applying filter effects

Now we have the shape, we'll add the waxy finish using the **Filter Effects**.

To add filter effects:

1. With the **Pointer Tool**, click to select the shape.

2. On the Drawing toolbar, click **Filter Effects**.

3. In the **Filter Effects** dialog, in the **Effects** list, click to select **Bevel and Emboss**.

4. Ensure that the preview window is closed so that you can see your updates in place on the page.

5. In the **Bevel and Emboss** section, set the **Style** to **Inner Bevel**. Drag the **Blur** slider to the right to increase the bevel effect (about 25 works well).

   We also increased the **Depth** slider to about **125**.

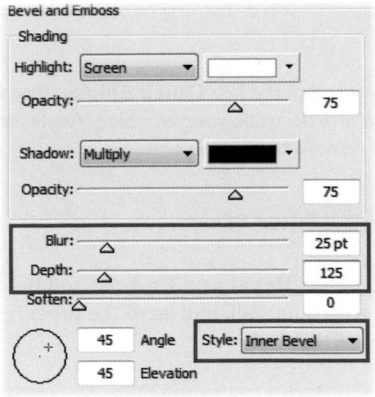

6. Click **OK**.

Don't forget to save your work!

Creating the seal

You can create anything you want, from a simple letter, to a more intricate combination of shapes and letters.

To create the centre ring:

1. On the QuickShapes flyout, click the **Quick Ellipse**, then hold down the **Shift** key and draw a circle inside your wax blob. Apply the same fill you used before and remove the outline.

2. On the Drawing toolbar, click **Filter Effects**.

3. In the **Filter Effects** dialog, select **Bevel and Emboss** and this time, simply increase the **Depth** to around **200** and leave the other settings at their default. Click **OK**.

4. With the **Pointer Tool**, click to select the circle and press **Ctrl+C** to copy it, followed by **Ctrl+V** to paste. The copied object is placed on top of the previous circle.

5. Press and hold **Ctrl** and **Shift** while resizing the top circle to make it smaller.

Holding the **Shift** key when resizing constrains the aspect ratio of an object. Holding the **Ctrl** key while resizing ensures that the centre position remains the same.

6. On the Drawing toolbar, click **Filter Effects**. This time, change the Bevel and Emboss **Style** to **Outer Bevel**. Change the **Angle** to **230**. Click **OK**.

We'll complete the design by using a single letter, 'x'.

To create the design:

1. On the Drawing toolbar, click the A **Artistic Text** button.

2. Click and drag on the page to set the size of the font to approximately **160** pt.

3. Type the letter 'X' and use the **Move** button to position the text in the centre of the inner ring.

4. With the **Pointer Tool**, click to select the text object and on the **Colour** tab, set the **Fill** to the same colour as you've used throughout.

5. On the Drawing toolbar, click fx **Filter Effects**. In the **Filter Effects** dialog, add an **Inner Bevel** with the following settings: **Blur:** 2; **Depth:** 150; **Angle:** 230.

Congratulations, you've created your first wax seal!

Don't forget to save your work!

As you can see, the entire process mainly consists of creating and manipulating QuickShapes and text objects, and then applying bevel and emboss effects to them.

Once you've mastered these techniques, you can create any design you want. Below are a couple of examples to get you started.

Torn Paper

In this tutorial, you will combine DrawPlus tools and techniques to make a variety of torn paper effects—including a pirate's treasure map.

By the end of this tutorial you will be able to:

- Draw lines and shapes with the **Pencil Tool**.
- Combine shapes using the **Subtract** command.
- Apply bitmap and gradient fills.
- Apply a drop shadow with the **Shadow Tool**.
- Apply a plasma fill to create a marble effect.
- Use the **Roughen Tool** to turn smooth edges into jagged outlines.
- Apply paper textures.

Let's begin...

- In the Startup Wizard, choose **Start New Drawing**, select a page size of your choice and click **OK**.

To create the shape:

1. On the Drawing toolbar, on the QuickShapes flyout, click the **Quick Rectangle** and draw a rectangle to represent your piece of paper.

2. On the Drawing toolbar, click the **Pencil Tool** and draw a jagged line to represent the torn edge of the paper.

Continue the line outside the edge of the rectangle and connect the start and end nodes to create a shape.

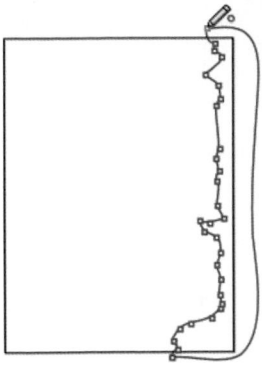

When you release the mouse button, your new shape will sit on top of the rectangle, hiding its edge.

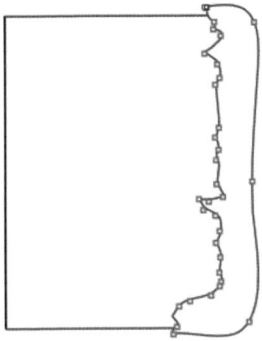

3. On the **Edit** menu, choose **Select All** (or press **Ctrl + A**) to select both the rectangle and the freehand shape.

4. On the **Arrange** tab, click the **Subtract** button. DrawPlus removes the section of the rectangle that is overlapped by the freehand shape.

Save now! Click **File > Save As...** and choose a new name for your file.

Now that we've got the basic outline for our piece of torn paper, there are a multitude of things we can do with it. We'll show you a few examples then we'll let you experiment on your own...

Adding a bitmap fill

To achieve this effect we applied one of DrawPlus's predefined bitmap fills to the shape, and then added a drop shadow.

To apply a bitmap fill:

1. With the **Pointer Tool**, click the shape to select it.

2. On the **Swatch** tab, click the arrow on **Bitmap** button and select **Misc** from the drop-down list.

3. Click the **Misc06** swatch to apply it to your shape.

4. On the **Line** tab, click **No line** to remove the shape's outline.

To create a drop shadow:

1. With the **Pointer Tool**, click the shape to select it.

2. On the Drawing Toolbar, click the **Shadow Tool**.

3. Click and drag down and slightly right to apply the shadow.

Creating a marbled effect

We can create a marble effect by applying and editing a plasma fill. This is a simple but effective technique.

To apply and edit a plasma fill:

1. With the **Pointer Tool**, click the shape to select it.

2. On the **Swatch** tab, click the arrow on the **Gradient** button and select **Plasma** from the drop-down list.

3. Apply any gradient fill by clicking its swatch.

4. With the shape still selected, on the Drawing toolbar, click the **Fill** tool. The shape's fill path and nodes display.

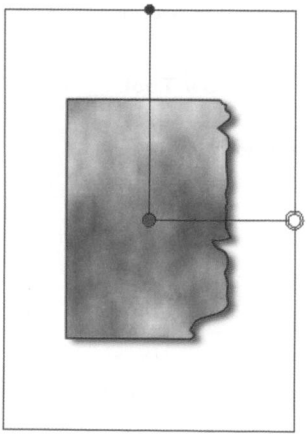

5. On the **Swatch** tab, click the arrow on the **Palettes** button and select a palette from the drop-down list.

6. Drag colour swatches from the tab to the fill path to change and add key colours. (We also removed the outline and applied a drop shadow to complete the page.)

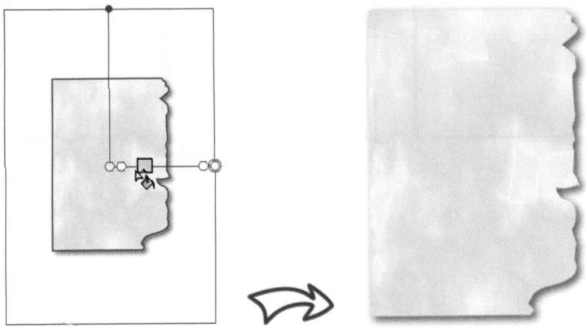

 **Don't forget to save your work!**

Creating a rough edge

The simplest method of all—we quickly roughened the edge of this piece of paper using the **Roughen** tool.

To create a rough edge:

1. With the  **Pointer Tool**, click the shape to select it.

2. On the Drawing toolbar, in the  Envelope Tools flyout, click the  **Roughen Tool**.

3. Click and drag either upwards or downwards. The further you drag, the more pronounced the effect. On release, the effect is applied.

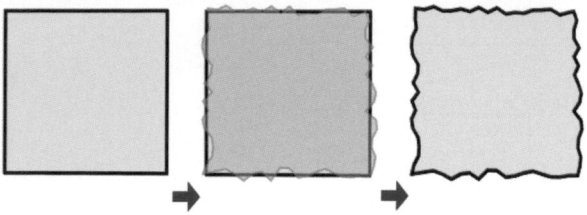

- Only the outline of the shape is affected and there's no internal distortion—so if you have applied a bitmap fill, for example, the fill remains intact.

- To remove a roughen effect from an object, double-click it with the **Roughen** tool, or click **Remove Roughen Effect** on the context toolbar.

Adding texture

DrawPlus provides you with a number of other fills and textures that are particularly suitable for creating paper effects.

Create a paper texture on the layer:

1. On the Layers tab, click **Apply Paper Texture**.

2. In the **Bitmap Selector** dialog, choose from the wide selection of textures available.

Create a paper texture on the object:

1. Create an exact copy of your paper object and paste it on top of the existing object.

2. On the **Swatch** tab, click the arrow on **Bitmap** button and select **Paper Textures** from the drop-down list. Try the various fills until you find a texture you like.

3. On the **Colour** tab, set the **Blend Mode** to **Screen**. The colour of the object beneath is revealed with the texture on top.

As you can see, once you have created the basic template for your torn paper, there are many things you can do with it. This tutorial has illustrated a few ideas, but we hope it has also inspired you to explore some of your own. We'll leave you with a final example.

Don't forget to save your work!

Example: Treasure map

Here we created a treasure map using a variety of DrawPlus tools and features. We'll explain how we did it; however, rather than replicating our example exactly, you should have fun with this and explore your own ideas!

Go to **http://go.serif.com/resources/DPX5** to download the following tutorial project file(s):

map.dpp

The individual elements of the treasure map are on **Layer 2** –you'll need to make **Layer 2** visible and hide **Layer 1**.

Burnt edge effect

fx We wanted the edges of our map to look charred. To accomplish this, in the **Filter Effects** dialog, we added an **Inner Glow** using the following settings:

- **Blend Mode**: Multiply
- **Opacity**: 75
- **Blur**: 30 pt
- **Intensity**: 15
- **Colour**: Mid brown—RGB(128, 80, 47)

Trees

We drew our two trees with the **Pencil Tool**, connecting the start and end nodes to make a closed shape. Each tree is made up of two shapes with a line and fill colour. The shapes were then **grouped**. The various groups of trees are simply copies, resized or flipped as necessary.

Scrub grasses

The grasses were created using the **Freeform Paint Tool** and we then applied a line and fill colour.

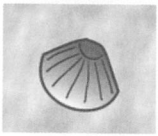

Shells

The shell was initially created with the **Quick Shield**. This was converted to curves and then edited with the **Node Tool**. (See *Shapes II: Modifying Shapes* on p. 43 for details.) We applied a gradient fill to add interest and added some line detail with the **Pencil Tool**. The grouped object was then copied, flipped, resized or rotated as necessary to create additional shells.

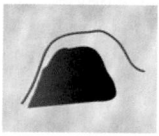

Caves

For the cave entrances, we used the **Pencil Tool**, connecting the start and end nodes to make a closed shape. We then applied a gradient fill to the shapes.

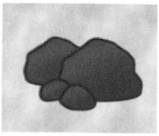

Rocks

The rocks were initially created with the **Quick Cloud**. This was converted to curves and then edited with the **Node Tool**. (See *Shapes II: Modifying Shapes* on p. 43 for details.) We applied a gradient fill to add interest.

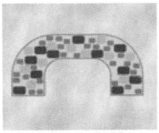

Bridge

 We used a **Quick Corner** to create one half of the bridge, then copied and flipped it. Finally, we added the two halves together with the **Shape Builder Tool**. The stones are **Quick Rectangles** with rounded corners.

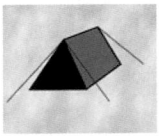

Tents

 We used the **Straight Line Tool**, connecting the start and end nodes to make a closed shape. Each shape was given a solid colour fill. The campsite was made up of copies of this first tent.

Flowers

 We made these with simple **Quick Petals**. The stems were drawn with the **Straight Line Tool**, and the leaves are **Quick Ellipses**.

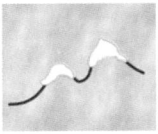

Mountains

 We used the **Pencil Tool** to draw the mountain range. The snowy peaks were created as separate objects using the **Freeform Paint Tool**.

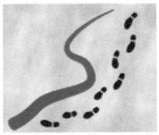

River and paths

 These were drawn with the **Pencil and Paintbrush Tools**. The river is a simple curved line. We applied a pressure gradient on the **Pressure** tab to give it some perspective. For the footpaths, we used a foot print style brush, "shoes", that we created for the map. (See *Creating Brushes* on p. 91 for more information on how to do this.)

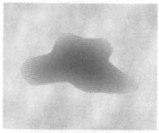

Water

To create the water we used the **Freeform Paint Tool**. We added depth to the water by applying a white, Inner Glow in the **Filter Effects** dialog.

Pirate Ship

A combination of shapes, lines, and fills was used to create our pirate ship with the **Pencil Tool**.

Fish

We used a **Quick Ellipse** and **Quick Shield** which we joined with the **Shape Builder Tool** to create the body, and added the top fin using the **Freeform Paint Tool**. The **Pencil Tool** was used for the details, and two **Quick Ellipses** for the eye.

Dragon

Our friendly dragon was created with the **Pencil Tool**, closing the shapes and applying fills where needed.

Shark

Our shark fin was created with the **Pen Tool**. We also added a few waves to hide the bottom of the filled shape.

Wine Glass

In this tutorial, we'll create a wine glass you can place on any background to show its transparency. This tutorial assumes that you are familiar with the main drawing and editing tools in DrawPlus. To help you with this more advanced project, we've created sample objects for you included in the resource file supplied with this tutorial.

By the end of this tutorial you will be able to:

- Turn a basic line drawing into a realistic 3D image.
- Apply simple fills and transparencies using the **Swatch** and **Transparency** tabs.
- Use the **Transparency Tool** to adjust the transparency of an object.

Go to **http://go.serif.com/resources/DPX5** to download the following tutorial project file(s):

glass.dpp

Let's begin...

- On the Standard toolbar, click **Open**.
- Locate the **glass.dpp** file and click **Open**.

The first page of the document shows a **keyline** (line drawing) of the wine glass, and the last page the finished article. The 'in-between' stages are shown on pages 2-5. If you look at the **Layers** tab for each page, you'll notice that the layers are named according to the stage.

To navigate between pages, click the **Previous Page** and **Next Page** buttons on the HintLine toolbar.

Save now! Click **File > Save As...** and choose a new name for your file.

Getting started:

1. On the HintLine toolbar, click the **Page Manager** and delete pages 2 to 6.

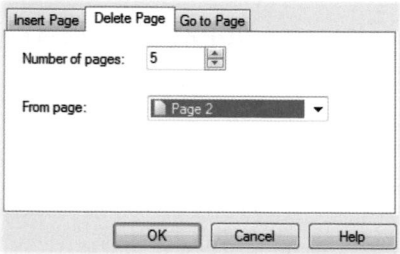

Save your changes.

2. Reopen the original file and keep it available for reference while you're working on the new file (use the **Window > Tile** command or adjust the windows for convenience).

Creating the Bowl

For this tutorial we'll remove any elements that aren't required, and bring it all together at the end. We'll begin with the top of the glass and work our way down. Since the wine glass is in keyline form to start with, you will only be able to select an element by clicking on the line itself.

To create the basic bowl:

1. In the **Layers** tab, select the 'Keyline' layer. Click the keyline of the 'bowl'.

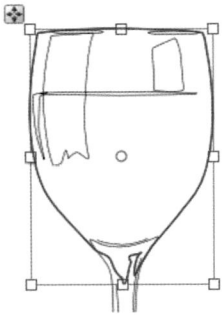

- On the **Colour** tab, apply a black fill and a set the **Opacity slider** to **10%** opacity.

- Remove the keyline (outline)—on the **Line** tab select **No Line**.

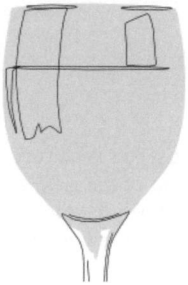

2. Select the left 'strip glow' and colour it solid white. Remove the keyline.

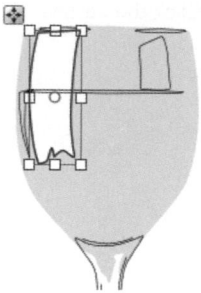

3. On the **Transparency** tab, in the **Gradient** drop-down list, select **Radial** and apply a radial transparency (we used **Radial 21**). Use the **Transparency Tool** to adjust the transparency so its path looks like our illustration (**A/1**).

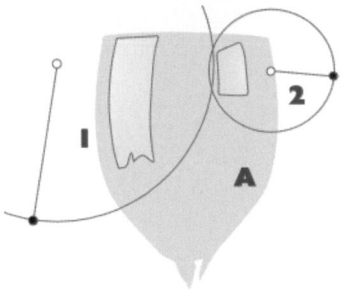

4. Repeat step 2 and 3 for the smaller strip glow (**A/2**).

See glass.dpp, Stage 1 (Page 2) for the completed steps.

5. Copy the longer strip glow and paste it over itself—this trick gives a sharper transparency. Do the same with the small strip glow, but after pasting it, nudge it slightly down and to the left. This will give the glass depth, as if light is also reflecting from the inside.

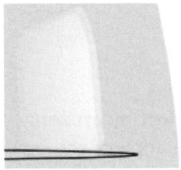

6. Select the main bowl, copy and paste it, then give it a white fill and increase the opacity to **20%**—it will be nearly invisible but that's the effect we want. Make it slightly smaller by pressing **Ctrl** while dragging inward on a corner handle.

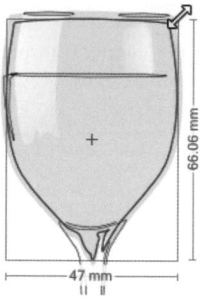

The bowl shape should now sit in front of the other bowl, leaving a slightly darker edge. This should give a glass a believable outline. In the following illustration, we've given the shape a false outline to illustrate its position.

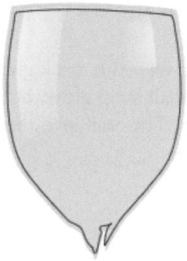

Next, we'll use this new bowl to enhance the glass effect by creating various transparency effects. Each time, we'll create a copy of the bowl object we create and use the copy as the basis for the following step.

Don't forget to save your work!

To enhance the glass effect:

1. With the new bowl object selected, apply the **Ellipse 19** transparency.

2. Click the **Transparency Tool** and drag the centre transparency node to position the transparency outside the object's right edge, slightly overlapping it to create a feathered soft edge.

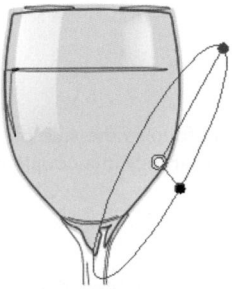

In the overlap zone, you should see a blending into white where less transparency reveals the new bowl's white colour. We'll duplicate this object and adjust the transparency on each copy to extend the feathered edge.

3. Copy and paste the new bowl, then drag its transparency zone up and adjust the nodes so that it resembles our screenshot.

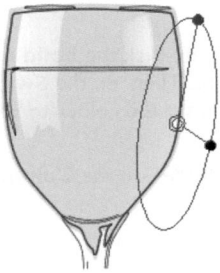

4. Copy and paste again, and this time, adjust transparency so that it covers the upper portion of the bowl.

Now you'll see a consistent white blend that follows the side of the glass. We'll use the same 'bowl' to add transparency in a couple of other areas.

The affect of the blend is more obvious on a darker background. On the **Layers** tab, click to show the 'background' layer to see this for yourself. Make sure that you hide it again afterwards.

5. Copy and paste again. This time we will create a white keyline for the inner bowl.

- Remove the fill colour—on the **Swatch** tab, click to select the **Fill** swatch and then click the **None** swatch.
- Apply a solid white line—on the **Line** tab, click the **Solid Line** button and set the line thickness to **1** pt. Then, on the **Swatch** tab, click to select the **Line** swatch and set the colour to white.
- Ensure that the line opacity is set to **100%**—on the **Colour** tab, drag the **Opacity slider** to the far right.
- Apply the **Ellipse 20** transparency.

6. Drag the transparency (not the object!) up to the top left area, as illustrated, and reshape it slightly to produce a light-reflective keyline that adds definition.

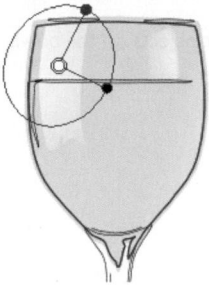

7. Copy and paste the newest bowl (with the amended keyline), and nudge the copy over to the right. Enlarge the transparency gradient, and position it to the right as we have done to create a stronger line down the side of the glass.

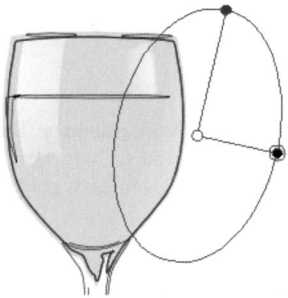

See glass.dpp, Stage 2 (Page 3)

Don't forget to save your work!

The next few operations are more of the same, in that we're adding a few more reflective transparencies—but these will be small 'flares' around the rim, front, side, and base of the glass.

To add the bowl accents:

1. In the **Layers** tab, select the 'Accents' layer.

2. With the **Pointer Tool**, select the accent objects on the bowl.

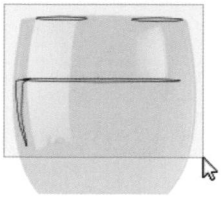

3. Remove the line and apply a white fill.

4. Apply an elliptical transparency from the **Transparency Tool** context toolbar and make adjustments as required so that the transparencies resemble our illustration (we've given each gradient a different colour to help you see what's going on).

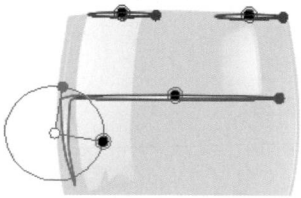

5. Finally select the single line just above the stem and change the line colour to white. Apply an elliptical transparency and modify it so that it resembles our illustration. This will define the base of the bowl.

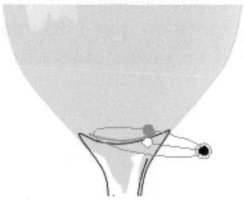

Against a coloured background, you should now have something closely resembling our illustration!

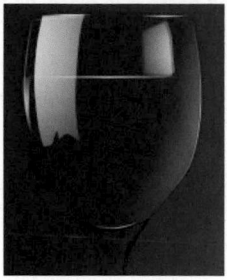

See glass.dpp, Stage 3 (Page 4). To display the background, simply make the 'background' layer visible.

Don't forget to save your work!

Creating the Stem

Now we'll follow similar procedures for the base and stem. The basic approach is to apply a light base colour and then side highlights, followed by the flares to add realism. We'll concentrate more on speed than detail, to avoid repetition. Don't forget to remove keylines unless otherwise stated.

To create the stem:

1. On the **Layers** tab, hide the 'Accents' layer. Select the 'Keyline' layer and then select the keyline that defines the stem. On the **Line** tab, click **No Line**. Next, on the **Colour** tab, click **Fill** and apply a black fill and reduce the opacity to **10%**. Copy and paste it in place, fill the copy with white, and add a **1** pt white line.

2. Using our illustration as a guide, apply an elliptical transparency to the object and move the transparency (not the object) to the right of the stem, with a slight overlap.

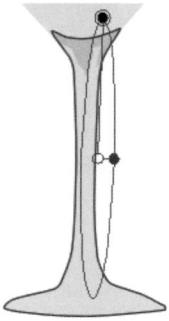

3. Copy the object and paste it again, so it retains its white fill and line, then rotate and extend the transparency to resemble our illustration. This will give the base of the stem a reflective glow.

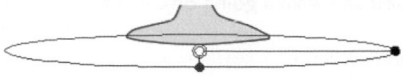

See glass.dpp, Stage 4 (Page 5).

Don't forget to save your work!

To finish off we'll apply the flares to the stem.

To add the stem accents:

1. On the **Layers** tab, make the 'Accents' layer visible and ensure that it is selected.

2. With the **Pointer Tool**, **Shift**-click to select each of the accent lines and change the colour to white and increase the line width to **1** pt.

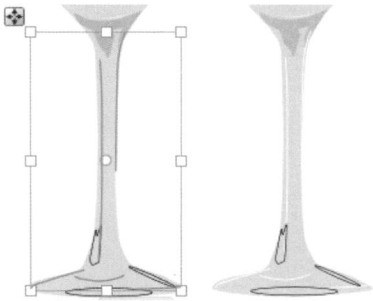

3. Apply either a radial or elliptical transparency to each line using the **Transparency Tool** context toolbar. Try to match the examples in the illustration below (we've given each gradient a different colour to help you see what's going on).

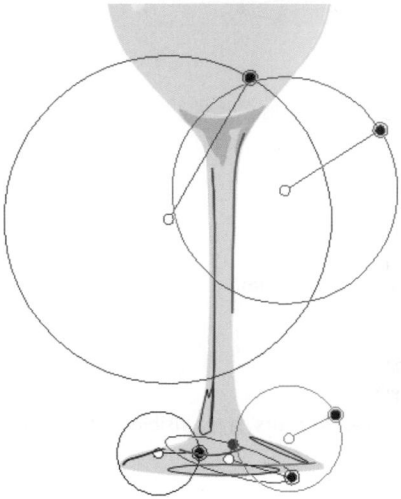

4. With the **Pointer Tool**, **Shift**-click to select the remaining three shapes. Remove the line and apply a white fill. Reduce the **Opacity** to **40%**.

5. Apply either a radial or elliptical transparency to each shape using the **Transparency Tool** context toolbar. Try to match the examples in the illustration below (we've given each gradient a different colour to help you see what's going on).

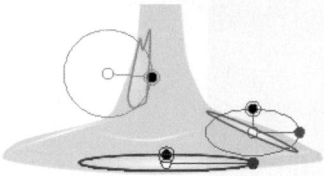

See glass.dpp, Stage 5 (Page 6). To display the background, simply make the 'background' layer visible.

Don't forget to save your work!

Congratulations! Your glass is complete. All you need to do is add a coloured background to complete the effect. To do this, we created a layer called 'background' and then added a QuickShape that covered the whole page. We applied a gradient fill to the QuickShape and... voila!

Now that you've mastered this technique, why not try applying the same methods to other objects like glass buttons for your website; or use the skills you've learned to create shiny metallic objects and water effects.

Creating Navigation Buttons

When you hover over a navigation button on a website, you'll often see that button change its appearance in some way to tell you that it's a button. So, how do designers do this? Well, it's all controlled by a clever bit of code and different graphics known as **rollover states**. Not a programmer? That's fine as DrawPlus creates all of the code for you, you just need to create the design!

By the end of this tutorial you will be able to:

- Create slice objects.
- Set button properties and states.
- Preview your finished web button in a web browser.
- Apply actions to buttons.
- Export your web button and its rollover states.

So that we can get straight to the business end of creating a 'rollover' navigation button, we have created the starting button for you.

Go to **http://go.serif.com/resources/DPX5** to download the following tutorial project file(s):

button.dpp

Let's begin...

- On the Standard toolbar, click **Open**.
- Locate **button.dpp** and click **Open**.

For this project, we have used a custom page setup with the ruler units set to pixels. Setting a specific page size is a good habit to get into when you are designing for a particular output such as for web buttons, icons and even logos. For more on changing ruler units and setting page size, see DrawPlus Help.

Save now! Click **File > Save As...** and choose a new name for your file.

Creating a web object

A rollover button is simply an image that has different states which are triggered by a mouse-over action or with a mouse click. Luckily, it's really easy to create these states in DrawPlus.

As you can see, we have created a "recycle" button graphic using a collection of different objects. These objects will become our starting image for our rollover button, known as the Normal rollover state, i.e., the appearance of the button when there is no mouse action taking place.

The next step is to change the graphic into a web object. To do this, we need to create a sliced object.

To create and adjust a sliced object:

1. On the **Insert** menu, click **Web Object>Image Slice**.

2. With the cursor, click and drag over the button to set the approximate size of the slice object.

On release, slice lines are displayed on the page defining the button as a separate web object.

On the **Layers** tab, you will notice that a new **Web Layer** has been created.

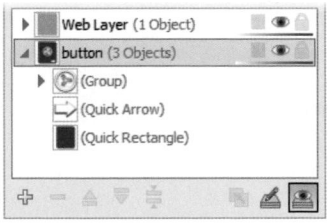

3. On the **Layers** tab, select the **Web Layer** and then, on the page, select the blue slice object with the **Pointer Tool**.

4. Drag the handles of the slice object so that they line up with the edges of the image.

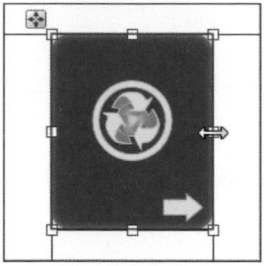

You can also insert a slice object from the right-click menu. Select your button first, and then on the right-click menu click **Insert Slice Object**. The slice area is immediately created at the correct size for the object. (Certain filter effects may cause the slice object to appear larger than the actual object dimensions due to the effect "bleed". In this case, you will need to adjust the slice manually.)

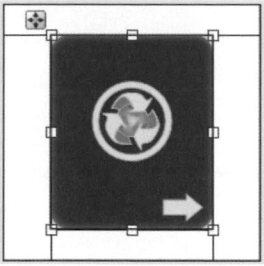

Don't forget to save your work!

Creating button 'states'

Now that our button is defined as a web object, we need to define its rollover states. This will allow us to apply different graphics to each state.

To define rollover states:

1. On the **Layers** tab, ensure that the **Web Layer** is selected and on the page, double-click the shaded region of the slice object. The **Image Slice Object Properties** dialog opens.

2. In the **Rollover Details** section, click to select the **Over** and **Down** check boxes and click **OK**.

3. On the **Layers** tab, you'll now see four layers in the document:

   - **Web Layer**—containing the image slice object.
   - **(Down)**
   - **(Over)**
   - **(Normal)**—containing the button.

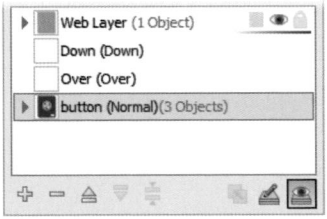

On the **Layers** tab, if you select the **Down** or **Over** layer, you'll see that they are empty. As we already have a graphic on our **Normal** layer, we can use this to create a **variant state** (a different graphic) on the **Over** and **Down** layers.

To create rollover states:

1. On the **Layers** tab, click to hide the **Web Layer**.

2. Click to select the 'button (**Normal**)' layer.

3. With the **Pointer Tool**, drag a selection around the entire button, and press **Ctrl** + **C** to copy.

4. On the **Layers** tab, select the **Over** layer. Press **Ctrl** + **V** to paste the copied objects. An exact copy of the objects is pasted in place.

5. Next, click to select the **Down** layer. Press **Ctrl** + **V** to paste the copied objects to this layer also.

   You should now have an exact copy of the button on each of the three 'state' layers (which you can see by expanding each layer as we have done).

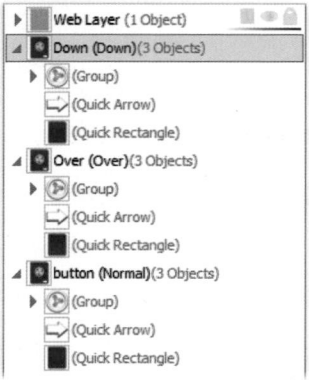

   At the moment, each state is an exact copy. So that something happens when we use our button, let's make a change to the **Over** state.

6. On the **Layers** tab, select the **Over** layer and then, click the grouped 'arrow' object.

7. Press the **Ctrl** key while dragging on a corner handle to increase the size of the object while keeping the centre in the same place.

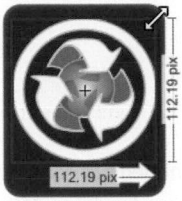

8. Click to select the QuickShape arrow at the bottom of the button, and on the **Colour** tab, adjust the colour wheel to apply an orange fill.

9. We'll leave the **Down** layer as it is so that the button returns to the same state when it is clicked.

Previewing a rollover button

Now that our three states are complete, we can preview the button in a web browser.

To preview a button:

1. On the **File** menu, click **Preview in Browser**. This launches your default browser and displays the button.

2. Roll your mouse over the button to see the variant 'Over' graphic you defined.

3. Close the browser window when you have finished previewing your button.

 **Don't forget to save your work!**

Applying actions (events) to a button

If you click the button in the browser, you may either receive an error message or notice no action takes place. This is because there is no URL link specified for the button. We'll show you how to set a link and specify some rollover text now...

To apply button actions:

1. On the **Layers** tab, select the **Web Layer** and click to make it visible.

2. Right-click the shaded region of the slice object and click **Properties...** The **Image Slice Object Properties** dialog opens.

3. In the URL details section:

   - Type a URL for your button to point to (for example www.recycle.com).

   - Type some descriptive text. This will appear when you point to the button. (For example 'Learn more about recycling'.)

   - Click **OK**.

4. Preview you button again to see the changes in action.

Don't forget to save your work!

Exporting your button

To complete the process of creating a web button, we need to export it. Let's do this now.

To export the complete rollover button:

1. On the **Web** layer, select the slice object and on the **File** menu, click **Export > Export as Image...**

2. In the **Image Export** dialog:

   - In the **Export Area** section, ensure **Selected Area** is selected.

   - In the **Properties** section, in the **Format** drop-down list, select an appropriate file type (typically GIF, JPEG, or PNG) and choose your settings. (We selected **32 bit PNG**).

   - In the **Web Options** section, ensure the **Image Slices** check box is selected.

   - Click **Export**.

3. In the **Export** dialog, select a location for your exported files (we recommend creating a folder first). Type a name for your button (e.g., btn) and click **Save**.

Congratulations, you've exported your web button along with its rollover states!

DrawPlus creates a file for each image state, and a single file containing the HTML code, from which you can copy and paste <head> and <body> sections into the corresponding sections of your web page.

If you now open your folder, the contents should resemble ours. (The appearance of the files depends on your settings and your current default browser—in our example, we have file extensions visible and the default browser is FireFox.)

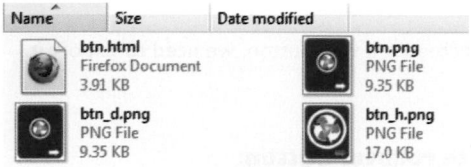

Serif WebPlus sites

If you own a copy of WebPlus, it's really easy to add your new navigation button to your website. From the **Insert** menu, click **DrawPlus Rollover...** In the dialog, browse to your exported button html file, select it and click **Open**. Finally, drag on the page to place your button object and **Preview** and/or **Publish** your page! For more information, see WebPlus Help.

To learn more about Serif WebPlus, see www.serif.com.

Introducing Animation

DrawPlus X5 provides exciting functionality that lets you create and export Adobe® Flash™-based animations using keyframes. Combine this with the extensive drawing capabilities of DrawPlus, and you have all the tools you need to create impressive movies, cartoons, Web banners, and so on.

In this reference tutorial, you'll learn about:

- Storyboarding.
- Starting the project and drawing the character.
- Cleaning up your sketch.
- Animating the character.
- Adding a background.

Introduction

The term **stopframe** (or **stop motion**) animation describes the conventional animation technique that makes static objects appear to move. The object is moved by very small amounts in successive frames, giving the impression of movement when the film is played.

In **keyframe** animation, a particular event or sequence of events is recreated in a series of snapshot images. The event is 'captured' at key moments (keyframes) where an object begins or ends an action. Animation between these keyframes is then calculated by the software—in this case, DrawPlus.

For example, suppose you want to create an animation of a bouncing ball. As the animator, you specify the start, end, and key intermediary positions of the ball, then DrawPlus smoothly fills in the gaps (a process known as **tweening**). At any point, you can fine-tune the animation to improve the duration, speed, and dynamics of the movement by adding or adjusting keyframes.

In the tutorials in this section, we will create both types of animation. In fact, within DrawPlus you can convert drawings (.dpp files) into both stopframe and keyframe animations, or you can take a stopframe animation file and use it to create a keyframe animation.

We'll now tell you a little bit more about how to go about creating an animation from scratch. However, if you want to just get stuck in, we'll see you again in the next tutorial, *Stopframe Animation* on p. 183!

1: Storyboarding

A storyboard is a visual script of the shots and scene changes in a video or film—a plan that you can refer to as you work on your project.

The storyboarding process helps you to think about how you want your finished animation to look, how the story should unfold, and how best to convey your story to your audience.

Think about what you actually want to achieve, and then create a rough illustration of what will happen during the animation. You don't have to be an artist—rough sketches and stick figures will do just as well.

2: Starting the project and drawing the character

The way you create your character is quite personal. Some designers prefer to sketch their rough ideas with pencil and paper first, while others prefer to work directly with the DrawPlus drawing tools. We suggest you experiment with both techniques to see which you prefer.

- If you're sketching with DrawPlus tools, we recommend you use **QuickShapes** for drawing simple shapes, the **Pencil Tool** for drawing freeform lines and shapes, and the **Pen Tool** for precise lines.

- You can fine-tune any line or curve by switching to the **Node Tool** and then adjusting the nodes and curves.

- If you have a drawing on paper that you'd like to use as the basis for your animation, scan it into your computer, save it as a graphics file, and then clean it up in DrawPlus. For information see the tutorial *Lines: Using the Pen Tool* on p. 75.

- If you're using a pen and tablet but are not too sure of your freehand drawing ability, you can place a printed image on the tablet and trace around its outlines.

To keep your Flash files as small as possible, you should generally avoid using special effects such as filter effects, shadows, 3D, transparency, bitmap fills, and so on, which are also output as bitmaps.

You can achieve some great simple 'hand-drawn effect' animations with the **Paintbrush Tool**. However, you should try to avoid using brushes if you intend exporting your project to Flash format. This is because brushstrokes are output as bitmaps and will result in a large file size.

3: Cleaning up your sketch

When you have created your rough sketch, the next task is to clean up the outlines and shapes. During this stage, you also want to identify and isolate the components that will be moving independently—if you do this, you'll find it easier to adjust and manipulate these parts as you work on your animation keyframes later.

These components will vary depending on your character and story, and will range from the obvious—for example, body, legs, head—to the not so obvious (eyebrows, ears, hair, lips, and so on). Don't go into too much detail at first though. Often, the simpler characters are the most effective, and you can always add more detail later if necessary.

The following tips will help you to achieve the best results:

- If you're working from a scanned image, place your original sketch on Layer 1, add a new layer and then work on this layer as you carefully trace over the original lines. When you've finished, hide the layer containing the original sketch to check your results. See the tutorial *Lines: Using the Pen Tool* on p. 75 for more details.

- Use **QuickShapes** for simple shapes. See the tutorials *Shapes I: Drawing with QuickShapes* and *Shapes II: Modifying Shapes* on p. 7 and p. 43, respectively, for more details.

- When using the **Pencil Tool**, increase the **Smoothness** on the context toolbar. This reduces the number of nodes on the line, resulting in a 'clean,' smooth running animation.

- **Group** your items - You'll be able to move and rotate all the objects in the group at the same time. You'll find this useful when you are animating the project.

- If you need to rotate a component or group of components that are 'hinged' from a fixed point—a leg, arm, or head for example—you'll achieve a more realistic effect if you move the centre of rotation to the hinge point.

To do this, select the object or group and then click and drag the **rotation origin** to the desired position. You can then rotate the object from a corner selection handle. The illustration below shows how we could use this technique to rotate the head of our cartoon dog.

When drawing your character:

- Keep it simple and use clean lines and shapes. You can create a detailed version first, to get a good feel for your character, but before you start animating it, you'll need to simplify it. The simpler your character is, the easier it will be to animate.

- Keep your colours simple and in blocks rather than random lines. This will make it easier for you to blend the moving elements of your drawing, and will also help minimize your final file size.

- Use shadows to 'ground' and add depth to your animation. Without shadows, your characters will appear to float.

- If your character is going to talk, you'll need to draw variations of the mouth for different 'sounds.' If you don't require too much detail, you can get by with a few basic mouth shapes—A, E, I, O, U, F, M, P, S, TH, and so on. You'll also need some transition shapes to take you from one mouth form to the next.

- You may need to move small body parts individually at times, but you'll save yourself a lot of effort by creating groups of parts that you can move and rotate together.

4: Animating the character

When you are happy with your character, you're ready to animate it. Our running dog example uses only 3 keyframes, but complicated animations may have many more. Keyframes (and stopframes) are displayed as frames in the storyboard tab.

Go to **http://go.serif.com/resources/DPX5** to download the following tutorial project file(s):

dog.dpa

When you **Preview** your animation, you'll see that the dog runs at a constant speed as the animation loops.

5: Adding a background

You may not need or want a background for your animation. It all depends on your subject matter and the final effect you want to achieve. In some cases, a background will reduce the impact of the scene.

A background will provide 'context' for your character, but can also be useful for adding perspective and depth to a scene. There are several ways to do this, for example:

- Use strong (saturated) colours for your character and foreground, and less strong (unsaturated) colours for background objects.

- Make foreground elements sharp and clear and your background elements blurred.

Backgrounds don't have to be detailed. In this racehorse storyboard, the roughly-sketched background gives the impression of motion and speed.

That's all there is to it! Now you know the principles, the next step is to start animating... Good luck!

Stopframe Animation

Turn a cartoon into an animation using the traditional stopframe animation technique.

By the end of this tutorial you will be able to:

- Clone animation frames.
- Create a basic animation by manipulating elements.
- Preview and export your animation.

We have created a Stopframe animation file that contains a single frame with the fish drawing for you to animate.

Go to **http://go.serif.com/resources/DPX5** to download the following tutorial project file(s):

cartoon.dpa

Let's begin...

- On the Standard toolbar, click **Open**.
- Locate the **cartoon.dpa** file and click **Open**. The first frame of the animation is displayed in the workspace.

Animating the cartoon

Now we are going to animate the fish. This requires us to copy and change individual frames to create the animation. Don't worry, you won't need to draw anything! Instead, we are going to use DrawPlus to clone our animation for us.

To clone a frame:

1. At the bottom of the workspace, you'll see Frame 1 displayed in the **Frames** tab.

If you can't see the **Frames** tab, click the **Open/Close** tab button at the bottom of the workspace.

2. On the **Frames** tab, click **Clone Frame** DrawPlus creates an exact copy of the first frame and opens it in the workspace.

Next, we need to animate the fish. We are going to use a technique called **Onion Skinning** to view our frame-by-frame changes.

Save now! Click **File > Save As...** and choose a new name for your file.

To animate frame 2:

1. On the Drawing toolbar, click the **Pointer Tool**. Click and drag to select the fish and the bubbles.

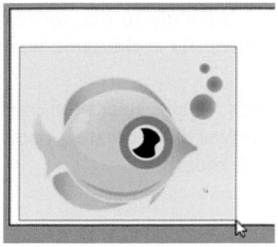

2. Press the right arrow key 10 times to move the fish to the right.

3. Click the **Onion Skinning** button. Notice that you can now see the first frame beneath the current frame. This allows us to check how much each element has moved.

Now let's animate the fish. In each frame, we are going to make some minor adjustments to the following:

- The upper fin
- The lower fin
- The bubbles

4. Select the upper fin and drag it downwards slightly so that more of it is hidden by the body. Hide part of the lower fin in the same way.

5. Select the bubbles and drag them upwards. Finally, select the smallest bubble, press the **Ctrl** key and drag downwards to create a copy. Position this new bubble nearest the fish's mouth.

Click the **Onion Skinning** button again to turn onion skinning off to ensure that you are happy with your frame.

Don't forget to save your work!

Creating additional frames

Here are some tips when creating the rest of the animation frames:

- Clone the most recent frame after making the adjustments.
- Select all of the elements and move them to the right with the arrow key. Move the elements by the same amount to create smooth movement.
- Animate the fins and the bubbles as in the previous steps, adding extra bubbles where necessary.
- Repeat the procedure until the fish reaches the other side of the screen (we used 12 frames).

- **Optional:** When your fish reaches the other side of the screen, select all of the elements and click **Flip Horizontal** on the **Arrange** tab.
- Repeat the clone and move process to get your fish to swim back across the screen.

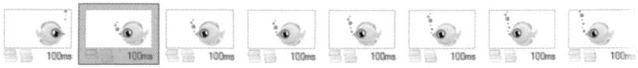

Don't forget to save your work!

Previewing and Exporting

Before you can show off your animation, you'll need to export it to a file! We recommend that you preview in DrawPlus first to make sure that the animation is exactly right before you take the time to export it

To preview the animation:

- On the **Frames** tab, click **Preview**.
- Click **Close** to exit the preview.

Our fish is swimming a little too quickly. We can change this by making each frame last a little longer. This is done by editing the frame properties.

To change the frame properties:

1. On the **Frames** tab, click **Properties**.
2. In the **Animation Properties** dialog, increase the frame display time to **150** milliseconds (ms) and click **OK**.

   All of the frames are updated.

To export the animation:

1. On the **Frames** tab, click **Export**.
2. In the **Export Optimizer** dialog, accept the default settings for **Animated GIF** and click **Export**.
3. In the **Export** dialog, type a name for your animation, choose a save location and click **Save**.

That's it! You can now view your creation by double-clicking to open it. Why not try animating some of your own DrawPlus creations?

Keyframe Animation

In this tutorial, we are going to create a fish tank complete with some swimming fish. Along the way, you'll learn about the special properties of keyframe animation, and how it can be used to animate objects without you having to draw every single frame.

By the end of this tutorial you will be able to:

- Insert a movie clip.
- Use keyframes to animate an object.
- Use an object envelope to add realism to movement.
- Use the AutoRun feature to automatically update object creation and placement as you work.
- Use a mask to hide unwanted areas.
- Export to .swf format.

Go to **http://go.serif.com/resources/DPX5** to download the following tutorial project file(s):

tank.dpa

Let's begin...

- On the Standard toolbar, click **Open**.
- Locate **tank.dpa** and click **Open**. The first frame of the animation is displayed in the workspace.

Importing animated clips

In the first frame of the animation, we've created a background that will serve as our fish tank. Of course, you can't have a fish tank without fish, so let's add some! We've created the fish for you, but you could always use your own...

The fish used in this tutorial was created using the techniques specified in the tutorial *Stopframe Animation* on p. 183. It was then converted to keyframe animation using the option in the **File** menu.

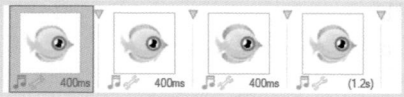

Finally, the fish was exported as a .swf file.

Go to **http://go.serif.com/resources/DPX5** to download the following tutorial project file(s):

fish.swf

If you want to import animations that you've already created, you'll need to import the .swf file. In DrawPlus, all previously created animations are known as "movie clips".

To insert a movie clip:

1. We want to add our movie clip to a new layer. On the **Layers** tab, click **Add Layer**.

2. Click the new layer to select it.

3. Go to **Insert > Movie Clip...**

4. Locate **fish.swf** and click **Open**.

5. Position the cursor on the grey pasteboard, just outside the top of the page and click once to place the movie clip at its default size. The clip displays the first frame.

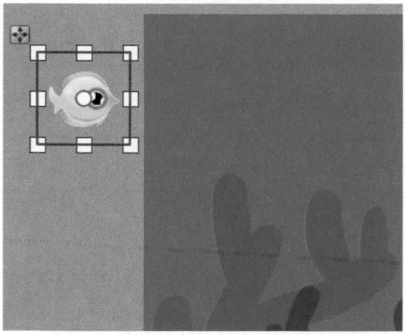

Save now! Click **File > Save As...** and choose a new name for your file.

Animating with keyframes

If we now preview the animation, the fish won't appear as it is not placed on the main page. We can use this to our advantage when making the fish 'swim' across the tank from one side to the other. We can do this by adding keyframes.

To add keyframes:

1. On the **Storyboard** tab, click **Insert**.

2. In the **Insert Keyframes** dialog, in the **Number of keyframes** box, enter **9**. Click **OK**.

   The inserted keyframes are displayed in the **Storyboard** tab.

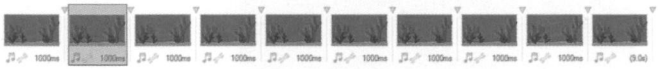

Click on any of the frames in the **Storyboard** tab. Notice that they are exact copies of the first frame you created. This makes it much easier to animate the objects. Let's now make the fish swim across the tank.

To animate the fish:

1. On the **Storyboard** tab, click to select the last frame in the sequence.

2. With the **Pointer Tool**, drag the fish clip to the pasteboard on the right of the tank background. Notice the path and light-grey nodes showing the movement of the fish?

   These represent the position of the automatically generated **motion tween** at each keyframe.

3. On the **Storyboard** tab, click to select the fifth frame in the sequence. Notice how the fish jumps to the corresponding node as it follows the motion tween.

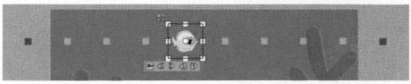

4. To preview your animation, on the **Storyboard** tab, in the **Preview** drop-down list, click **Preview in Flash Player**. You should now see the fish swimming at a constant speed in a straight line across the tank.

Now that our fish is swimming across the tank, we can edit each keyframe to make the fish swim in a more interesting pattern. Let's do this now.

Don't forget to save your work!

To edit keyframes:

1. On the **Storyboard** tab, click to select the fifth frame in the sequence.

2. With the **Pointer Tool**, drag the fish clip down towards the bottom of the tank. Notice how the path and nodes update in the other keyframes.

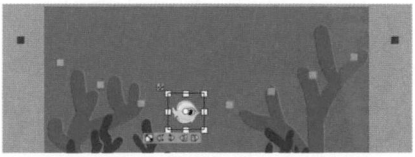

3. Click **Preview** to preview the animation.

4. On the **Storyboard** tab, click to select the seventh frame in the sequence. The node representing keyframe 5 has turned dark grey. This is because it is now a **key object**—in other words, you have

defined that the fish must be in that position on that frame. Tweened objects are automatically generated by DrawPlus.

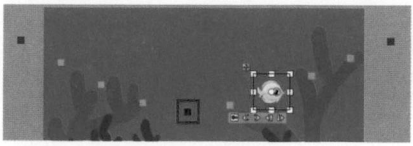

5. With the **Pointer Tool**, drag the fish clip upwards slightly. Notice that the path between frames 1 and 5 does not change as it is set between two key objects.

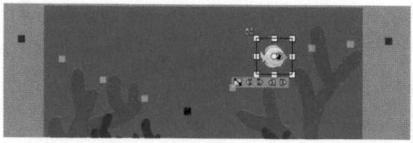

6. Click **Preview** to preview the animation. You should see your fish swimming across the screen following the path you specified.

When you preview your animation, you'll see that the fish moves at a constant speed throughout the entire animation. This may be the effect you require, but suppose you want to vary the speed of an object as it moves through a scene? Read on!

Don't forget to save your work!

Adjusting object envelopes

When you select an object that is part of a 'run sequence' (such as one of the fish), the **Easing** tab becomes available.

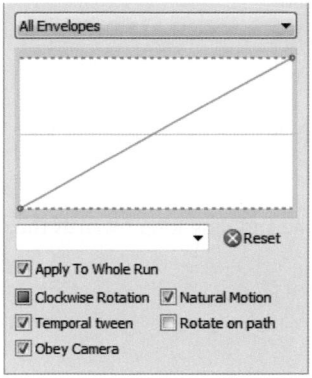

In DrawPlus keyframe animations, the **Easing** tab provides a drop-down list of **envelopes** (Position, Morph, Scale, Rotation, Skew, Colour, and Transparency). These envelopes work in similar ways to control how an object's properties change over time, from keyframe to keyframe. Once you learn how to display and modify one type of envelope, you can apply the same principle to the others.

By default, DrawPlus applies a constant rate of change to all envelopes, but you can adjust this by modifying the envelope profile settings.

In this section, we'll make the fish appear to change speed as it swims through the tank by applying and modifying a **position envelope**.

To apply a position envelope:

1. Open keyframe 1 and select the fish clip.

2. On the **Easing** tab, expand the Envelopes drop-down list and select the **Position Envelope**.

   Below the drop-down list, in the Envelope Profile pane, the blue diagonal line represents the rate of change of the fish's position from this keyframe to the next.

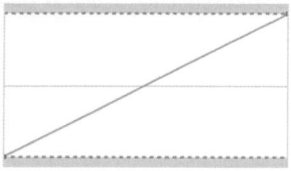

By default, the rate of change is constant, but we can change this by adjusting the gradient of the profile.

3. Click a point in the middle of the blue line and drag it up towards the top of the pane.

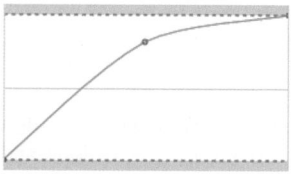

4. Notice that the nodes on the downward curve start off quite far apart and then get closer together.

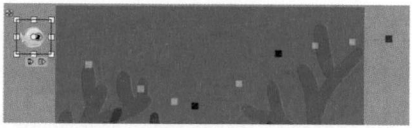

5. Preview your animation again. You should see the fish swim into the tank quickly and then slow up as it reaches the bottom of the curve (where the nodes get closer together) and then, swim off at a constant speed.

Don't forget to save your work!

Using AutoRun

To stop our fish from being lonely, let's add another!

To insert a clip using AutoRun:

1. Click the **AutoRun** button to enable this feature. By default, any new objects you create or reposition on any keyframe will now automatically run to the end of the storyboard.

2. Select keyframe 1 and then, go to **Insert > Movie Clip...**

3. Locate **fish.swf** and click **Open**.

4. Position the cursor on the grey pasteboard on the opposite side to the first fish click once to place the movie clip at its default size.

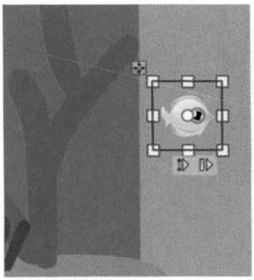

If you now take a look at your storyboard, you'll see that DrawPlus has placed a copy of the fish in all subsequent keyframes.

5. On the Standard toolbar, click **Flip Horizontal**.

6. On the toolbar beneath the clip, click the **Update attributes forwards** button. In the dialog, ensure **To end of storyboard** is displayed and click **OK**. Your second fish will now be facing left throughout the animation.

7. Click the **AutoRun** button to disable this feature. Now you're ready to animate the path of the fish as you did with the first example!

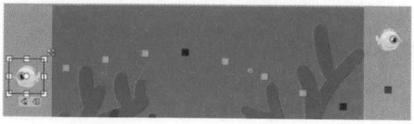

Don't forget to save your work!

Masking unwanted areas

If you're happy with your animation, you're almost ready to export it. However, because our animation goes outside the page, if it was resized, you'd see the fish swimming outside the tank.

We can easily fix this by adding a **mask**.

To add a mask:

1. On the **Layers** tab, click **Add Layer**. Rename the new layer 'Mask'.

2. Select the first frame. Working on the **Mask** layer, click the **Quick Rectangle** and draw a rectangle that covers the page. On the **Swatch** tab, apply a bright colour to the fill and outline.

   This rectangle shape will act as a 'window'.

3. On the **Transform** tab, set the exact dimensions to **854** pix wide by **480** pix high.

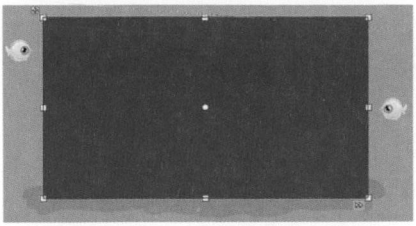

4. On the **Align** tab, click **Centre Horizontally** and **Centre Vertically**.

5. On the toolbar beneath the rectangle, click **Run placement forwards**. In the dialog, ensure **To end of storyboard** is displayed and click **OK**. Your rectangle will now appear throughout the animation.

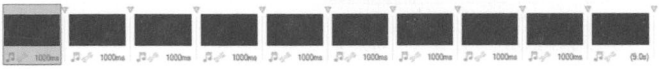

6. On the **Layers** tab, right-click the **Mask** layer and click **Layer Properties...** In the **Layer Properties** dialog, in the **Attributes** section:

   - Select the **Locked** check box.

   - Select the **Mask** check box and then in the drop-down layers list, select **2**.

This tells DrawPlus that we want this layer to mask both layers. (If we'd chosen to mask 1 layer, the mask would not hide objects on the **background** layer.)

- Click **OK**.

7. On the **Layers** tab, the Ⓜ **Mask** and 🔒 **Locked** icons now display next to the **Mask** layer. The colour of the layers also change to clearly show the mask layer and the layer being masked.

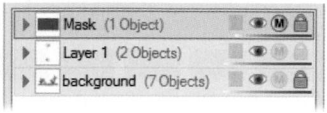

Until you lock a mask layer, the mask object, and the objects outside of the mask area will show on the page. As soon as the layer is locked, it becomes transparent and all objects outside of the mask are hidden from view.

8. As soon as the mask is locked, only the objects within the mask area can be seen—if you open frame 1, you'll see that the fish appear to have disappeared. Don't worry, they are only hidden as you can see by clicking through each frame.

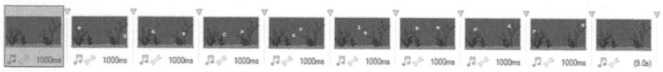

9. Preview your animation and resize the window to see the mask in action!

Don't forget to save your work!

Exporting your animation

You can export to the following formats:

- Adobe Shockwave Flash file (.swf)
- Video (choose from .mov, .stv, .avi, .wmf file formats)
- Screensaver (.scr)
- Flash Lite/ i-Mode (a lightweight version of .swf, optimized for viewing on mobile phones and other devices)
- Image (a wide range of formats are supported, see DrawPlus Help for details)

For this project, we will export our animation to a standard Shockwave Flash .swf file.

To export to Adobe Shockwave Flash:

1. On the **File** menu, point to **Export** and then click **Export as Flash SWF...**.
2. Choose a file name and save location for your .swf file and then click **Save**.
3. The **Keyframe Animation Export** dialog displays the progress of the export and closes when export is complete.

   Simply browse to locate the file and then double-click to open it.

We hope that you have enjoyed working through this project and are happy with the resulting animation. Don't forget, you can add as many fish as you want! Why not insert them on later frames so they appear at different times?

We hope that you are now comfortable with the basics of keyframe animation and are ready to begin experimenting with your own projects. Have fun!

DrawPlus Gallery

This chapter showcases the content provided on the DrawPlus X5 **Gallery** tab. You'll find layout symbols, connecting symbols, shape art, and even more clipart! Also, new in X5, is the web section.

Gallery items are organised into the following categories:

- British ClipArt Collection
- ClipArt
- Home
- Office
- School
- ShapeArt
- Web

The **Gallery** tab also lets you store your own designs in a **My Designs** section if you would like to reuse them—the design is made available in any DrawPlus document.

Food & Drink

Apple Pie

Apple

Asparagus

Aubergine

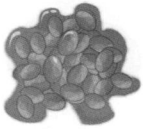

Baked Beans

Bakewell Tart

Bangers And Mash

Battered Sausage

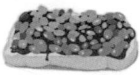

Beans On Toast

Beetroot

Blackberries

Black Pudding

Blueberries

Bottle of Wine

Bread

Bread Roll

Broad Beans

Broccoli

Brown Sauce

Burger Sauce

Butter And Toast

Brussels

Cabbage

Candy Floss

Carrots

Cauliflower

Celery

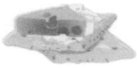
Cheese and Cream Crackers

Cheese and Pineapple on stick

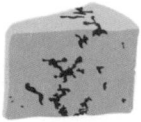
Cheese

Chicken Tikka

Chocolate Orange Cake

Christmas Pudding

Christmas Dinner

Cider

Courgette

Cranberries

Crisps

Crumble

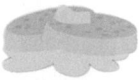
Crumpets

Cumberland Sausage

Cup of Tea

Custard

Damson

Dandelion & Burdock

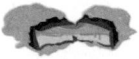
Deep Fried Choc Bar

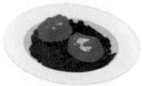
Dumplings

Dundee Cake

Elderberries

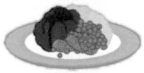
Faggots

Fish and Chips

Full English Breakfast

Gin and Tonic

Ginger Beer

Gingerbread

Gravy

Haggis

Honey Jar

Honeycomb

Ice Cream

Irish Stew

Jam Strawberry

Jam Sandwich

Jellied Eels

Jelly and Ice Cream 1

Jelly and Ice Cream 2

Kebab

Ketchup

Kippers

Lager

Lancashire Hot Pot

Leek

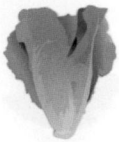

Lettuce

Marrow

Mayo

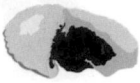

Mince Pies

Mint Sauce

Mustard Pot

Pasty

Pear

Peas

Pickled Onion on Stick

Pint of Ale

Pint of Dark Ale

Ploughman's Lunch

Plums

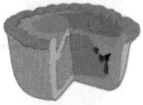

Pork Pie

Pork Scratchings

Potato

Pumpkins

Radish

Raspberry

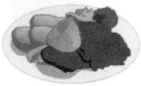

Roast Dinner

Roly Poly Pudding

Rowan Berries

Runner Bean

Sandwich

Sausage Roll

Sausage On Stick

Scone

Scotch Broth

Scotch Egg

Shepherds Pie

Shortbread

Soup And Crusty Roll

Spinach

Spotted Dick

Spring Onions

Staffordshire Oatcakes

Stick Of Rock

Strawberry

Sweet Potato

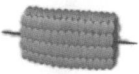

Sweetcorn

Tatties

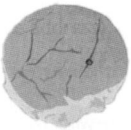

Teacake

Teapot

Toad In The Hole

Toffee Apple

Tomato

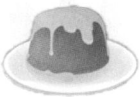

Treacle Pudding

Turnip

Victoria Sponge

Watercress

Yorkshire Pudding

History

Army Truck

Canon

Cenotaph

Crown 01

Crown 02

Crown 03

Crown 04

Crown Jewels

Helmet

Infantryman's Sword

Pirate Ship

Pirate Sword

Plague Rat

Proverb - Bird In The Hand

Proverb - Cracked Bell

Proverb - Early Bird

Proverb - Every Cloud

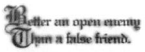

Proverb - False Friend

Proverb - Friend Indeed

Proverb - Has An Art

Proverb - Mice Will Play

Proverb - Old Dog

Proverb - Cracked Bell

Poppy Wreath

Poppy

Soldier

Trenches

Landmarks & Buildings

10 Downing Street

Allotment

Angel of the North

Apartments

Balmoral Castle

Ben Nevis

Big Ben

Big Ben With Flag Backdrop

Blackpool Tower

Blarney Castle

Brighton Pier

Buckingham Palace

Bungalow

Canal Bridge

Canterbury Cathedral

Castle 1

Castle 2

Castle 3

Castle Bridge

Cerne Abbas Giant

Church

Cottage

Eden Project

Edinburgh Castle

Flats

Gherkin

Glastonbury Tor

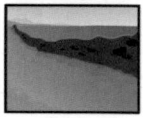
Hadrian's Wall

House of Parliament

Iron Bridge

King College Cambridge

Lake District

Lands End

Lighthouse

Loch Ness Monster

Log Cabin

London Guildhall

Long Man of Wilmington

Mansion with Gates

Marble Arch

Millennium Bridge

Millennium Dome

Pier

Post Office

Public House

Sandringham

Sign Underground

Stately Home 1

Stately Home 2

St Paul's Cathedral

Stonehenge

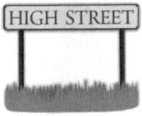

Street Sign

Terraced

Thames Bridge

Tower Bridge

Tower of London

Trafalgar Square

Tyne Bridge

White Cliffs of Dover

White Horse of Uffington

Windmill

Windsor Castle

York Minster

Objects

Arcade Machine

Bagpipes

Bowler Hat

Christmas Decorations

Christmas Tree

Cult Boots

Currency

Firefighter Helmet

Flares

Garden Gnome

Hat and Scarf

Keep Britain Tidy

Light Bulb

Maypole

Mini Skirt

Mod Symbol

Pocket Watch

Post Box

Quill

Retro TV

Rosette

Scarecrow

School Boy Uniform

School Girl Uniform

Slot Machine

Space Hopper

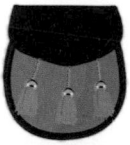
Sporran

Stile

Telephone Box

Toaster

Top Hat

People

60's Pop Band

Adventurer

Artist

Baker

Beefeater

British Paratrooper

Butcher

Christopher Columbus

Churchill

Civil Servant

Cricket Player

Dickens

English Gent

English Holiday Goer

Explorer

Farmer

Female Writer

Fireman

Fisherman 1

Fisherman 2

Fishmonger

Football Fan

Football Player

Francis Drake

George And The Dragon

Glastonbury Hippies

GP

Graduate

Guy Fawkes

Headmaster

Henry Viii

Highwayman

Irish Guard

Judge

King Arthur

King and Queen

Leprechaun

Lollipop Lady

Maid

Milkman

Morris Dancer

Naval Officer

Nightclubbers

Nun

Nurse

Peasant

Pilgrim Father

Pirate

Policeman

Popstar

Prime Minister

Punch And Judy

Punk

Richard The Lionheart

Rob Roy

Robert Burns

Robin Hood

Royal Guard

Royal Marine

Rugby Player

School Teacher

Scots Guard

Shakespeare

Sleuth

St Andrew

St David

Tennis Player

Vicar

William Wallace

Youth

Plants

Ash Tree

Birch Tree

Bluebell

Buttercup

Cedar Tree

Clover

Clovers

Conker

Cowslip

Daffodils

Daisy

Dandelion

Dandelion Seed Head 1

Dandelion Seed Head 2

Deadly Nightshade

Doc Leaf

Elderflower

Elm Tree

Evening Primrose

Fern

Forget-me-not

Fox Glove

Foxtail

Gorse Branch

Grass

Hawthorn Berries

Heather

Hemlock

Holy

Holly Branch

Honey Suckle

Hornbeam

Horse Chestnut

Ivy

Maple Tree

Mistletoe

Nettles

Oak Tree

Parsley

Passion Flower

Pine Tree

Poplar

Poppy

Primrose

Privet

Rhododendron

Rose 1

Rose 2

Rowan Tree

Silver Birch

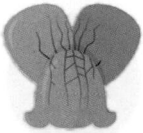
Snap Dragon

Spindle Branch

St Johns Wort

Sweet Briar

Sycamore

Thistle

Willow Tree

Yew

Sports & Outdoors

Archery

BBQ

Beach Huts

Bucket and Spade

Badminton

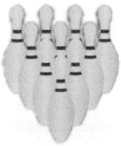
Bowling

Camping

Chess

Croquet

Darts

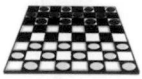
Draughts

Equestrian

Fishing

Football

Formula One

Frisbee

Greyhound Racing

Horse Racing

Paintball

Ping Pong

Playing Cards

Polo

Pool

Rambling

Rowing

Rugby League

Skateboard

Snooker

Table Tennis

Tennis

Tent 1

Tent 2

Twickenham

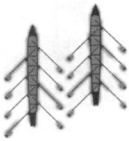

University

Transport

3 Wheeled Car

Ambulance

Black Cab

Canal Boat

Chopper

Classic Car 1

Classic Car 2

Classic Car 3

Classic Motorbike

Classic Race Car

Classic Train

Cycle

Digger

Double Decker 1

Double Decker 2

English Trawler

Harrier Jump Jet

Helicopter

Highwheel Bicycle

Horse And Cart

Hot Air Balloon

Lancaster Bomber

Mary Rose

Milk Float

Motorbike

Penny Farthing

Police Car

Ambulance

Red Arrows

School Bus

Scooter

Ship

Speed Camera

Spitfire

Submarine

Superbike

Tank 1

Tank 2

Tank 3

Titanic

Tractor

Tram

Trike

White Van

Wildlife

Ant

Badger

Bass

Billy Goat

Blackbird

Blenny

Bloodhound

Blue Tit

British Bulldog 1

British Bulldog 2

Budgie

Bull

Bumble Bee

Carp

Cat

Chaffinch

Chick

Chicken

Cockerel

Cod

Coot

Corgi

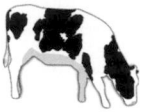
Cow

Cricket

Crow

Cuckoo

Deer

Dogfish

Donkey

Dove

Dragonfly

Duck

Eagle

Eel

English Terrier

Falcon

Field Mouse

Fox

Glow Worm

Goat

Goldfinch

Goldfish

Goose

Grey Squirrel

Grouse

Hamster

Hedgehog

Hawk

Heron

Hornet

Hoverfly

June Bug

Kingfisher

Labrador

Lamb

Magpie

Mayfly

Millipede

Mole

Monarchy Butterfly

Newt

Otter

Partridge

Peacock Butterfly

Peacock

Pheasant

Pig

Pigeon

Piglet 1

Piglet 2

Pike

Rabbit

Raven

Red Admiral Butterfly

Red Squirrel

Robin

Scottish Terrier

Seagull

Sheep

Shrew

Slug

Snowy Owl

Sparrow

Squirrel

Stag Beetle

Stag

Stickleback

Stoat

Swallow

Swallowtail Butterfly

Swan

Tawny Owl

Thrush

Trout

Turtle Dove

Wasp

Weasel

Woodpecker

Worm

Wren

Animals

Bird

Bumblebee

Cow

Crab

Crocodile

This is only a preview of this gallery category—there are more designs available in this category in the **Gallery** tab.

Birth

Baby

Bib for Boy

Bib for Girl

Bootie

Bottle

This is only a preview of this gallery category—there are more designs available in this category in the **Gallery** tab.

Christmas

Purple Bauble

Orange Bauble

Candy Cane

Christmas Tree

Decorated Christmas Tree

This is only a preview of this gallery category— there are more designs available in this category in the **Gallery** tab.

Easter

Easter Bunny

Easter Duckling

Egg Basket

Flowers

Fashion

Boots

Brush

Champagne Bottle

Champagne Glasses

Eyelash Brush

This is only a preview of this gallery category—there are more designs available in this category in the **Gallery** tab.

Food & Drink

01

02

03

04

05

This is only a preview of this gallery category—there are more designs available in this category in the **Gallery** tab.

Funny Faces

Army Helmet

Baby Bonnet

Brown Beard

Cowboy Bandanna

Cowboy Hat

This is only a preview of this gallery category—there are more designs available in this category in the **Gallery** tab.

Home & Garden

Hi-Fi

Radio

Screwdriver

Spanner

Speaker

This is only a preview of this gallery category—there are more designs available in this category in the **Gallery** tab.

Party

Balloon

Balloons

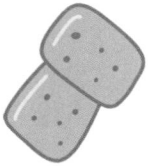

Bottle Cork

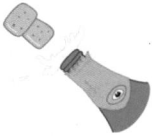

Champagne

Cupcake

This is only a preview of this gallery category—there are more designs available in this category in the **Gallery** tab.

People & Professions

Waitress

Police Officer

Superhero

Secretary

Girl

This is only a preview of this gallery category—there are more designs available in this category in the **Gallery** tab.

Romance

Cake

Cat

Cupid

Flower Cluster

Heart

This is only a preview of this gallery category—there are more designs available in this category in the **Gallery** tab.

Seasons

Clouds

Glove

Grass

Hat

Kit

This is only a preview of this gallery category—there are more designs available in this category in the **Gallery** tab.

Smilies

Angry

Cheeky

Cool

Crying

Duh

This is only a preview of this gallery category—there are more designs available in this category in the **Gallery** tab.

Sports & Leisure

8 Ball

Bowling Ball

Basketball

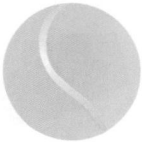

Tennis Ball

Soccer Ball

This is only a preview of this gallery category—there are more designs available in this category in the **Gallery** tab.

Transport

Boat

Bus

Car 01

Car 02

Forklift Truck

This is only a preview of this gallery category—there are more designs available in this category in the **Gallery** tab.

Wedding

Bells

Bouquet

Bride

Bridesmaids Dress

Cake

This is only a preview of this gallery category—there are more designs available in this category in the **Gallery** tab.

Vectors

Birds01

Birds02

Birds03

Birds04

Birds05

Birds06

Birds07

Birds08

Birds09

Birds10

Birds11

Birds12

Birds13

Birds14

Birds15

Birds16

Birds17

Birds18

People01

People02

People03

People04

People05

People06

People07

People08

People09

People10

People11

People12

People13

People14

People15

People16

People17

Branch01

Branch02

Branch03

Branch04

Branch05

Branch06

Branch07

Branch08

Branch09

Branch10

Branch11

Branch12

Branch13

Branch14

Branch15

Branch16

Floral01

Floral02

Floral03

Floral04

Floral05

Floral06

Floral07

Floral08

Floral09

Floral10

Floral11

Decorative01

Decorative02

Decorative03

Decorative04

Decorative05

Decorative06

Decorative07

Motif01

Motif02

Motif03

Motif04

Motif05

Motif06

Motif07

Motif08

Motif09

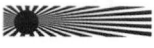
Motif10

Twirl01

Twirl02

Twirl03

Twirl04

Twirl05

Twirl06

Twirl07

Twirl08

Twirl09

Twirl10

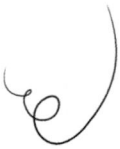
Twirl11

Twirl12

Twirl13

Twirl14

Twirl15

Twirl16

Twirl17

Twirl18

Twirl19

Twirl20

Twirl21

Twirl22

Twirl23

Scatter01

Scatter02

Scatter03

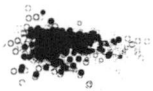

Scatter04

Scatter05

Scatter06

Scatter07

Scatter08

Scatter09

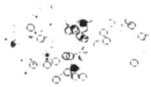

Scatter10

Scatter11

Pop01

Pop02

Pop03

Pop04

Pop05

Pop06

Pop07

Pop08

Pop09

Pop10

Aeroplane

Car

Family Tree - Connecting - Block

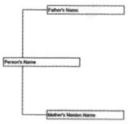

Pedigree

Pedigree_2

Pedigree_3

Pedigree_4

Pedigree_5

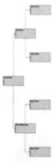

Pedigree_6

Family Tree - Connecting - Line

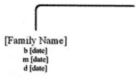

Extra Child Left

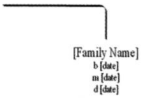

Extra Child Right

Family Name

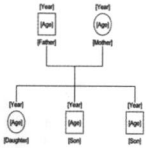

Family

Female

Male

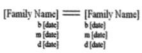

Marriage

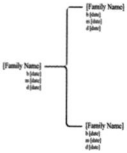

Pedigree_7

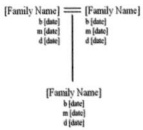

Single Child

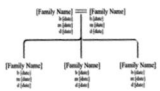

Three Children

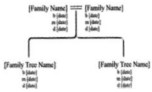

Two Children

Family Tree - Connecting - Photographic

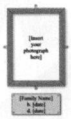

Frame and Nameplate

Frame and Nameplate_2

Single Frame

Single Frame_2

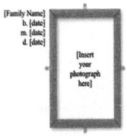

Single Photo Frame

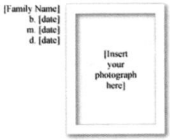

Single Photo Frame_2

Wooden Frame

Wooden Frame_2

Wooden Frame_3

Wooden Frame_4

Wooden Frame_5

Fun & Crafts - Badges

Rainbow

Skull

Boy

Girl

I Love You

Mod

Punk

Smile

Pop

Star

Rock

Flaming Bike

Seal

Dice

Butterflies

Flower

Fire

Car

Fun & Crafts - Printmaking

Coffee 1

Coffee 2

Coffee 3

Coffee 4

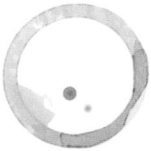

Coffee 5

Coffee 6

Wine

Tea

Splatt 1

Splatt 2

Splatt 3

Lips 1

Lips 2

Lips 3

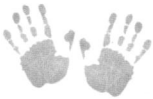

Hands

Paws 1

Paws 2

Bird 1

Bird 2

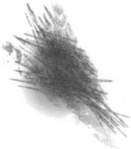

Grass 1

Grass 2

Grass 3

Fun & Crafts - Scrapbooking

Tag

Price

Pin

Yellow Note

Pin

Sticker

Price

Polaroid

Paper Clip

Paper

Pink Note

Yellow Note

Page Curl

Page Corner

Pin

Tag

Label

Paper

Note

Old Label

Tape Measure

Safety Pins

Buttons

Sequins

Jewels

Glass Beads

Flower Beads

Furry Teddies

Furry Sun

Furry Flowers

Furry Dogs

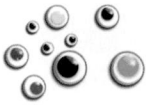

Boggly Eyes

Fun & Crafts - Stickers

Blue Stars

Party Rabbit

Sun Cocktail

White Rabbit

Party Cat

Orange Sweets

Strawberry Cream

Golden Rabbit

Mint Sweets

Ice Cream

Blue Cat

Vanilla Cream

Vanilla Cherry

Raspberry Radio

Red Rabbit

Marino Cherry

Raspberry Cat

Blue Radio

Sunset Cocktail

Star Cherry

Cherry Cream

Orange Cat

Blue Stars

Moon Light Cocktail

Garden Planning - Bedding

Bedding I blue

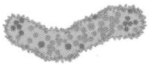

Bedding I mauve

Bedding I pink

Bedding I red

Bedding I white

Bedding 1 yellow

Bedding 2 bronze

Bedding 2 cool green

Bedding 2 dark green

Bedding 3 bronze

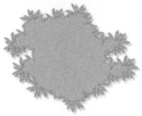

Bedding 3 cool green

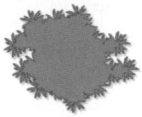

Bedding 3 dark green

Garden Planning - Buildings & Fixtures

Apex roof shed

Arbour

Brick wall section

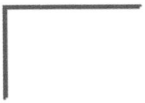

Brick wall with return

Bridge 1

Bridge 2

Cold frame

Fence panel and post - blue

Fence panel and post - brown

Fence panel and post - cedar

Fence panel and post - green

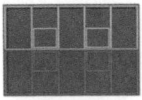

Medium greenhouse

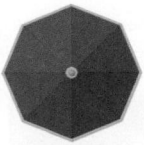

Octagon summerhouse

Pent roof shed

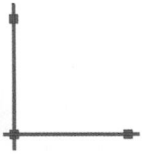

Pergola section - blue

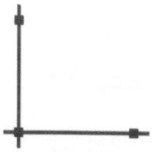

Pergola section - brown

Pergola section - cedar

Pergola section - green

Sentry box store

Small greenhouse

Summerhouse

Garden Planning - Containers

Container 1 black

Container 1 blue

Container 1 brown

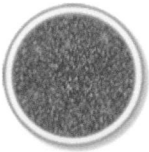

Container 1 cream

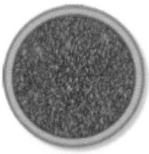

Container 1 grey

Container 1 terracotta

Container 2 black

Container 2 blue

Container 2 brown

Container 3 cream

Container 2 grey

Container 2 terracotta

Container 3 black

Container 3 blue

Container 3 brown

Container 3 cream

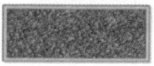

Container 3 grey

Container 3 terracotta

Container 4 black

Container 4 blue

Container 4 brown

Container 4 cream

Container 4 grey

Container 4 terracotta

Garden Planning - Furniture

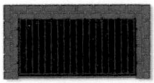

Barbecue

Blue patio chair

Blue patio table 1

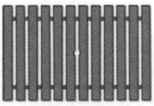

Blue patio table 2

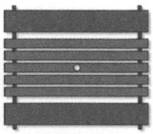

Blue patio table 3

Blue patio table 4

Blue patio umbrella

Garden seat

Gnome

Green patio umbrella

Kid's slide

Natural patio chair

Natural patio table 1

Natural patio table 2

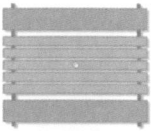

Natural patio table 3

Natural patio table 4

Sandpit

Teak patio chair

Teak patio table 1

Teak patio table 2

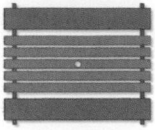

Teak patio table 3

Teak patio table 4

Terrace seating area - blue

Terrace seating area - natural

Terrace seating area - teak

Trampoline

Yellow patio umbrella

Garden Planning - Hedges, Shrubs & Trees

Hedge cool green

Hedge dark green

Large tree

Leylandii hedge

Medium tree

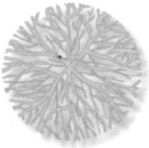

Shrub 1 cool green

Shrub 1 evergreen

Shrub 10 bronze

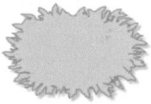

Shrub 10 cool green

Shrub 10 dark green

Shrub 2 bronze

Shrub 2 cool green

Shrub 2 dark green

Shrub 3 bronze

Shrub 3 cool green

Shrub 3 dark green

Shrub 4 bronze

Shrub 4 cool green

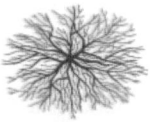

Shrub 4 dark green

Shrub 5 bronze

Shrub 5 cool green

Shrub 5 dark green

Shrub 6 dark green

Shrub 6 red-green

Shrub 6 silver grey

Shrub 7 cool green

Shrub 7 dark green

Shrub 7 yellow green

Shrub 8 blue

Shrub 8 mauve

Shrub 8 pink

Shrub 8 red

Shrub 8 white

Shrub 8 yellow

Shrub 9 bronze

Shrub 9 dark green

Shrub 9 pale green

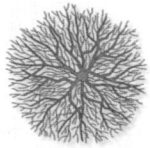

Small tree

Garden Planning - Surfaces & Features

Bark chip area

Bedding area 1

Bedding area 2

Bedding area 3

Bedding area 4

Bedding area 5

Bedding area 6

Bedding area 7

Border area 1

Border area 2

Border area 3

Border area 4

Coir matting section

Curved path section 1

Curved path section 2

Curved path section 3

Decking section blue

Decking section natural

Gravel area

Large pond 1

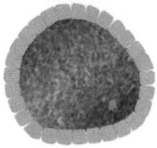
Large pond 2

Lawn 1

Lawn 2

Lawn 3

Lawn 4

Lawn 5

Lawn 6

Lawn 7

Lawn 8

Lawn 9

Lawn 10

Patio edging 1

Patio edging 2

Patio surface 1

Patio surface 2

Patio surface 3

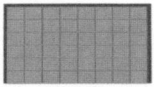

Patio surface 4

Patio surface 5

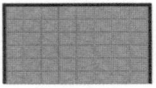

Patio surface 6

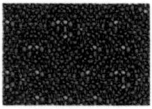

Pebble area

Rockery Corner

Rockery

Simple Stone Chippings

Small pond 1

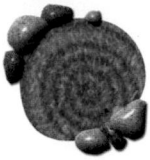

Small pond 2

Stone chippings area 1

Stone chippings area 2

Stone chippings area 3

Straight path section 1

Straight path section 2

Straight path section 3

Stream 1

Stream 2

White sand area 2

Interior Planning - Beds

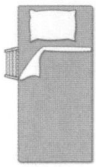

Bunk bed

Crib

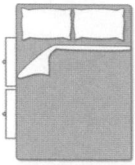

Double bed with drawers

Double bed

Futon bed as seat

Futon bed

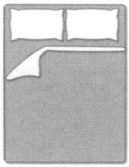

King Size bed

Single bed

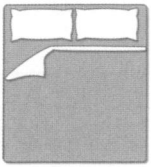

Super King Size bed

Interior Planning - Cabinets

Corner cabinet

Display cabinet

Long cabinet

Long Display cabinet

Small cabinet

Wide cabinet

Interior Planning - Kitchen Cabinets

12inch deep narrow wall...

12inch deep wall cabinet

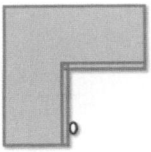

12inch deep wall LHS corner...

12inch deep wall RHS corner...

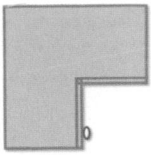

20inch deep wall LHS corner...

20inch deep narrow wall...

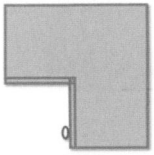

20inch deep wall RHS corner...

20inch deep wall cabinet

24inch deep floor cabinet

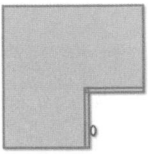

24inch deep floor cabinet LHS...

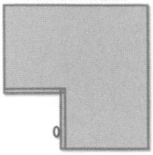

24inch deep floor cabinet RHS...

24inch deep narrow floor...

4 foot length worktop 01

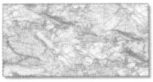

4 foot length worktop 02

4 foot length worktop 03

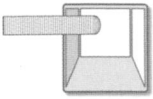

Extractor Hood 01

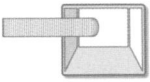

Extractor Hood 02

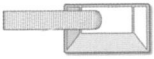

Extractor Hood 03

Interior Planning - Leisure

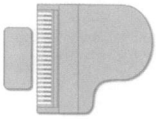

Baby grand piano

Billiards table

Grand piano

Micro HiFi system

Midi HiFi system

Music keyboard

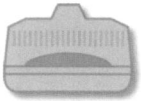

Portable TV

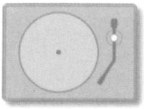

Record turntable

Standard HiFi system

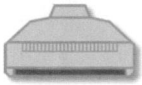

Standard TV

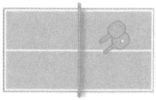

Table tennis table

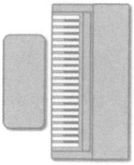

Upright piano

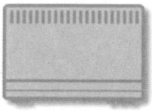

VCR-DVD

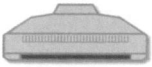

Widescreen TV

Interior Planning - Lighting

Ceiling lamp

Double spotlight

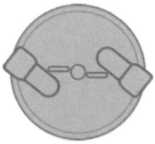

Floor lamp with spots

Floor lamp

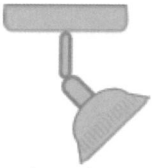

Low voltage spotlight

Low voltage track

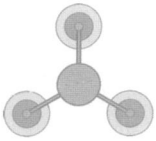

Pendant light

Single spotlight

Uplighter

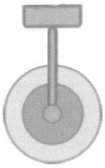

Wall lamp

Interior Planning - Major Appliances

Chest freezer

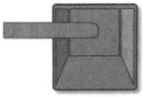

Cooker hood-extractor

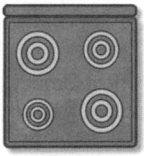

Cooker

Dishwasher

Five-zone hob

Four-zone hob

Microwave

Mini fridge

Range oven

Two-zone hob

Upright fridge-freezer

Washer or dryer

Interior Planning - Plumbing Fixtures

Belfast sink

Bidet

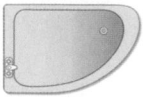

Corner bathtub

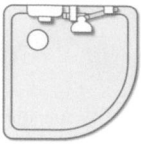

Corner shower 1

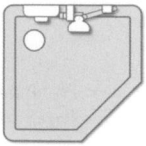

Corner shower 2

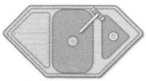

Corner sink

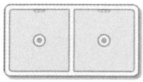

Double Belfast sink

Double drainer

Double sink with drainer

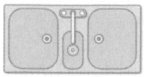

Double sink

Mixer Taps

Oval Bathtub

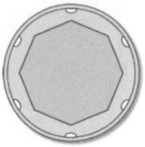

Round HotTub

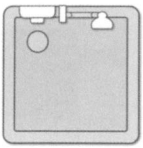

Shower cubicle

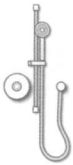

Shower head unit front-on

Shower head unit

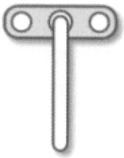

Sink mixer taps

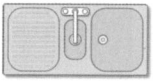

Sink with left drainer

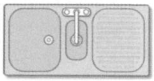

Sink with right drainer

Small bathtub

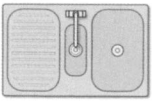

Spacesaver sink

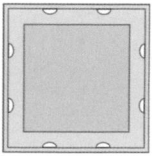

Square Hot Tub

Standard bathtub

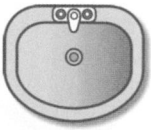

Standard washbasin

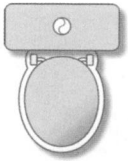

Toilet with cistern

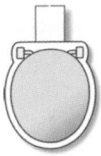

Toilet

Victorian bathtub

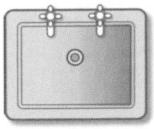

Victorian Washbasin

Walk-in shower

Interior Planning - Seating

Armchair

Carver chair

Centre unit

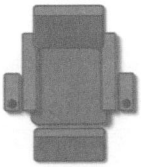

DeLuxe recliner

Dining chair

Futon bed as seat

Left corner unit

Modular seating

Modular table

Recliner

Right corner unit

Settle

Three-seater sofa

Tub armchair

Two-seater sofa

Interior Planning - Tables

4 place table

Oblong 6 place table

Oblong 8 place table

Oblong coffee table

Oval 4 place table

Oval 6 place table

Oval 8 place table

Oval coffee table

Round 4 place table

Round 6 place table

Round 8 place table

Round coffee table

Interior Planning - Walls, Doors &

12 foot wall

Bay window

Double doors

Double Floor Stairs

Double window

Single window

Spiral Staircase

Stairs

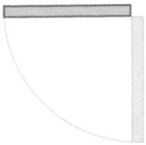

Standard door - left hand

Standard door - right hand

In the **Home** category you'll also find a **Technical Planning** section, containing layout symbols that can be used for technical layout plans. Categories in this section are as follows:

1 Building Fixtures
2 Cabinets
3 Cupboards
4 Gardens
5 Leisure
6 Lighting
7 Major Appliances
8 Office Furniture
9 Plumbing Fixtures
10 Seating
11 Tables

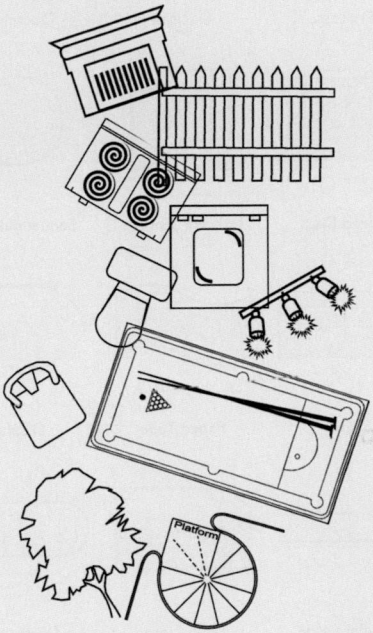

Flowcharts - Connecting - Designed

Process

Decision

Document

Data

Predefined Process

Stored Data

Internal Storage

Sequential Data

Direct Data

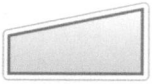

Manual input

Card

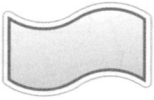

Paper Tape

Display

Manual Operation

Preparation

Parallel mode

Loop Limit

Terminator

On-page Reference

Off-page Reference

Flowcharts - Connecting - Outline

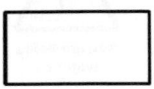

Process

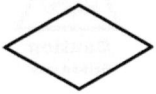

Decision

Document

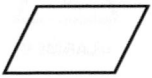

Data

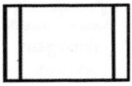

Predefined Process

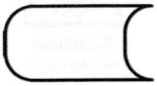

Stored Data

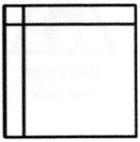

Internal Storage

Sequential Data

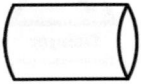

Direct Data

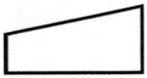

Manual input

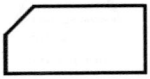

Card

Paper Tape

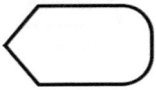

Display

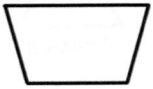

Manual Operation

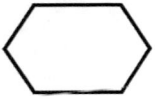

Preparation

Parallel mode

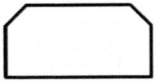

Loop Limit

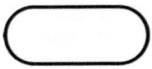

Terminator

On-page Reference

Off-page Reference

Health & Safety - Hazard

415 Volts

Alarmed

Asbestos

Barbed Wire

Being Watched

CCTV

Compressed Gas

Electric Shock

Fire Risk

Fork Lift Trucks

Harmful Chemicals

Hot Water

Lorries Reversing

Men Working Overhead

Mind the Step

Mind your Head

Oxygen Cylinder

Persons at Work

Proceed with Care

Radiation Risk

Radiation

Ramps

Video Surveillance

Warning

Wet Floors

Health & Safety - Mandatory

Angled Arrow

Arrow Up

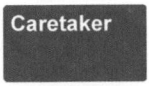

Caretaker

Cloakroom

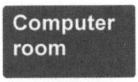

Computer Room

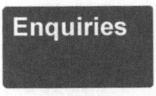

Enquiries

General Office

Keep Clear

Keep Out

Keep Shut

Library

Lift

Main Entrance

Meeting Room

Nursery

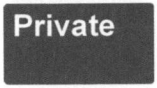

Private

Ramp

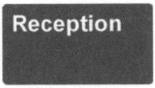

Reception

Report To

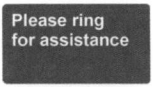

Ring for Assistance

Smoking Area

Smoking Room

Staff Only

Staff Room

Switch Off

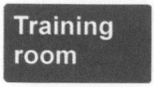

Training Room

Waiting Room

Warning Sign

Health & Safety - Misc

Accepted

Awaiting Inspection

Back Sign

Calibration

Car Park

Date Installed

Deliveries

Directional Arrow

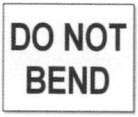

Do Not Bend

Employee Parking

Entrance

Fragile

Goods In

Handle with Care

ISO 9000

Keep Out

Private Parking

Private Property

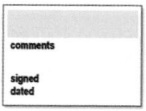

Quality Tested

Quarantine Area

Rejected

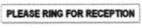

Ring for Reception

Switch Off

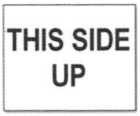

This Side Up

This Way Up

Urgent

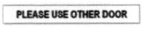

Use Other Door

Visitor Parking

Health & Safety - Prohibition

Cameras

Do Not Disturb

Fire Alarm

Fire Blanket

Left Arrow

Mobile Phone

Motorcycle

No Exit

No Food or Drink

No Pedestrians

No Smoking

Health & Safety - Standard

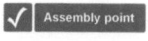

Assembly Point

Drinking Water

Eye Wash

Fire Exit 01

Fire Exit 02

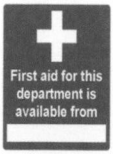

First Aid Available

First Aid Post

First Aid

First Aiders

Left Arrow

Phone

Pull to Open

Pull

Push to Open

Push

Smoking Area

Logos

Logo 01

Logo 02

Logo 03

Logo 04

Logo 05

Logo 06

Logo 07

Logo 08

Logo 09

Logo 10

Logo 11

Logo 12

Logo 13

Logo 14

Logo 15

Logo 16

Logo 17

Logo 18

Logo 19

Logo 20

Logo 21

Logo 22

Logo 23

Logo 24

Logo 25

Logo 26

Logo 27

Logo 28

Logo 29

Logo 30

Logo 31

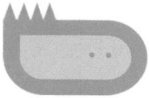

Logo 32

Logo 33

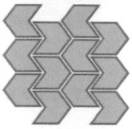

Logo 34

Logo 35

Logo 36

Logo 37

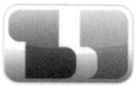

Logo 38

Logo 39

Logo 40

Logo 41

Logo 42

Logo 43

Logo 44

Logo 45

Logo 46

Logo 47

Logo 48

Logo 49

Logo 50

Networks - Connecting

Bridge

Camera

Cell Phone

Comm-link

Comm-link_2

CRT

CRT_2

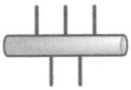

Ethernet

Fax

Firewall

Hub

Modem

PC Unit

Photocopier

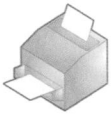

Printer

Projector

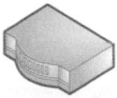

Router

Scanner

Screen

Switch

Telephone

TFT

User

Video Camera

Wireless Router

Wireless

Organisational Charts - Connecting

Badge

Badge_2

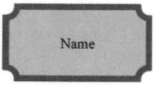

Badge_3

Badge_4

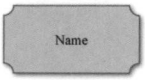

Badge_5

Badge_6

Badge_7

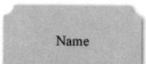

Badge_8

Circle

Circle_2

Circle_3

Circle_4

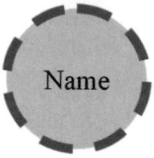

Circle_5

Circle_6

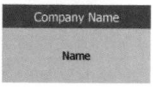

Company Name

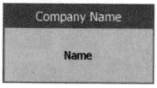

Company Name_2

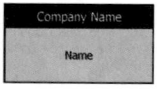

Company Name_3

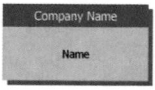

Company Name_4

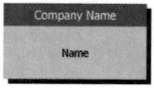

Company Name_5

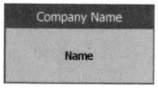

Company Name_6

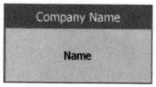

Company Name_6

Lozenge

Lozenge_2

Lozenge_3

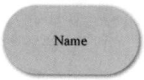

Lozenge_4

Lozenge_5

Lozenge_6

Oval

Oval_2

Oval_3

Oval_4

Oval_5

Oval_6

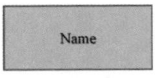

Rectangle_1

Rectangle_2

Rectangle_3

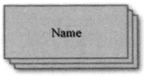

Rectangle_4

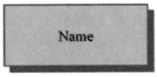

Rectangle_5

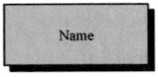

Rectangle_6

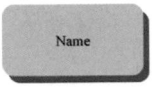

Rounded Rectangle

Rounded Rectangle_2

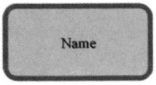

Rounded Rectangle_3

Rounded Rectangle_4

Rounded Rectangle_5

Rounded Rectangle_6

Design & Technology > Electronics

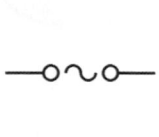

AC Supply

Aerial

Ammeter

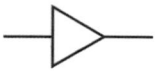

Amplifier

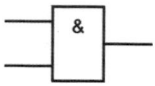

AND Gate (IEC)

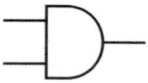

AND Gate

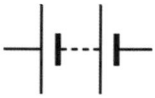

Battery

Bell

Buzzer

Capacitor

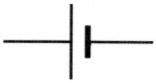

Cell

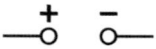

DC Supply

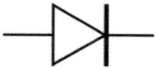

Diode

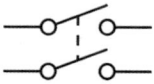

Dual On-Off Switch

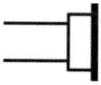

Earphone

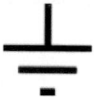

Earth

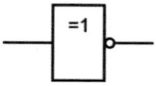

EX-NOR Gate (IEC)

EX-NOR Gate

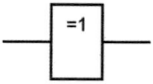

EX-OR Gate (IEC)

EX-OR Gate

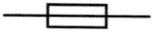

Fuse

Galvanometer

Ground

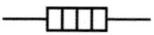

Heater

Inductor

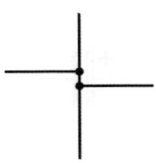
Join 01

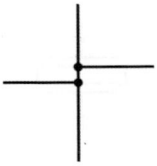
Join 02

Join 03

Join 04

Join 05

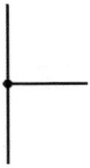
Join 06

Join 07

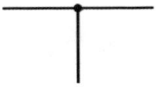
Join 08

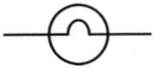
Lamp

Lamp_2

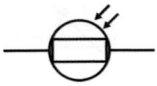
LDR

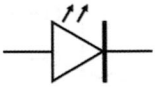
LED

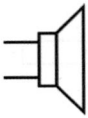
Loudspeaker

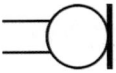
Microphone

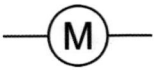

Motor

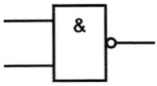

NAND Gate (IEC)

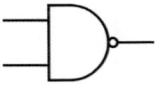
NAND Gate

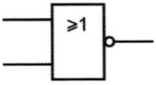

NOR Gate (IEC)

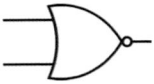
NOR Gate

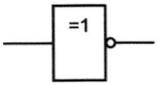

NOT Gate (IEC)

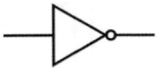
NOT Gate

Not Join 01

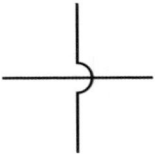
Not Join 02

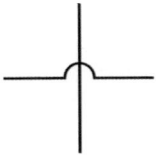
Not Join 03

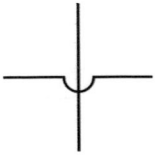
Not Join 04

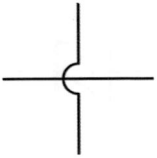
Not Join 05

Ohmmeter

On-Off Switch

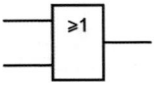

OR Gate (IEC)

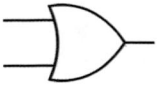
OR Gate

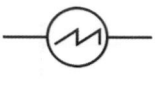

Oscilloscope

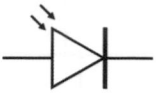

Photodiode

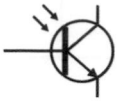

Phototransistor

Piezo Transducer

Polarised Capacitor

Potentiometer 02

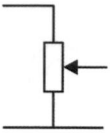

Potentiometer 03

Potentiometer Variable Resistor

Potentiometer

Preset Variable Resistor

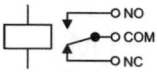

Relay

Resistor 02

Resistor

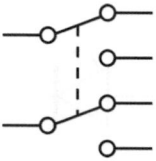

Reversing Switch

Rheostat Variable Resistor

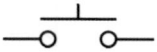

Switch

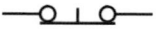

Switch_2

Thermistor

Timer Chip 555

Transformer

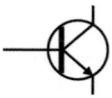

Transistor NPN

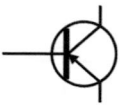

Transistor PNP

Trimmer Capacitor

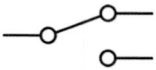

Two-Way Switch

Variable Capacitor

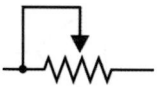

Variable Resistor 02

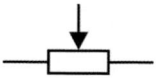

Variable Resistor 03

Variable Resistor

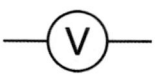

Voltmeter

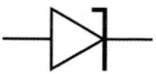

Zener Diode

Design & Technology > Food

Cake Knife

Chef Hat

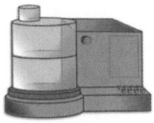

Food Processor

Handheld Mixer

Knife

Rolling Pin

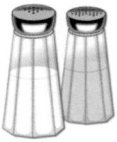

Salt & Pepper

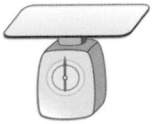

Scales

Spoon

Toaster

Wooden Spoon

Design & Technology > General

Cutting Board

Eraser

Hammer

Knife

Paintbrush

Pencil

Ruler

Saw

Scissors

Scraper

Stationery Stencil

Tape

In this Resource Guide, previews of the gallery category **Electronics - Connecting** are not shown.

Geography > Flags

Austria

Belgium

Cyprus

Czech Republic

Denmark

England

Estonia

European Union

Finland

France

Germany

Great Britain

Greece

Hungary

Ireland

Italy

Latvia

Lithuania

Luxembourg

Malta

Netherlands

Poland

Portugal

Scotland

Slovakia

Slovenia

Spain

Sweden

United States

Wales

Geography > Weather

Bright Slight Clouds

Clouds some Sunshine

Cloudy - Night

Cloudy

Dark Clouds with Rain - Night

Dark Clouds with Rain

Dark Clouds

Fog - Night

Hazy

Heavy Rain

Icy Blizzard - Night

Icy Blizzard

Lightening Storm - Night

Lightening Storm

Mild Sunshine

Showers - Night

Showers

Snow - Night

Snow

Sunny Showers

Very Sunny

Maths > Maths - Colour

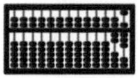

Abacus 01

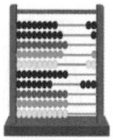

Abacus 02

pi

Protractor

Ruler

Set Square

Set Square 02

This category is also available as outlines in the **Gallery** tab.

Sciences > Biology > Diagrams - Colour

DNA

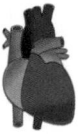

Heart

Intestines

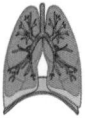

Lungs

Microscope

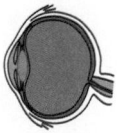

Retina

This category is also available as silhouettes in the **Gallery** tab.

Sciences > Chemistry > Laboratory

Beaker

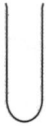

Boiling Tube

Bung

Bunsen Burner and Tripod

Bunsen Burner

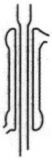

Condenser

Conical Flask

Crucible

Drying Tube

Erlenmeyer Flask

Evaporating Basin

Flat-Bottom Flask

Funnel

Glass Tubing 01

Glass Tubing 02

Glass Tubing 03

Glass Tubing 04

Glass Tubing 05

Large Test Tube

Measuring Cylinder

Round-Bottom Flask

Tap

Test Tube

Thistle

Three Way Adapter

Tripod

U-Tube

Volumetric Pipette

Watch Glass

Sciences > Chemistry > Symbols - Colour

Beaker

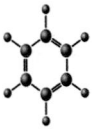

Benzene

Burette

Clamp

Conical Flask

Dropper

Evaporating Dish

Graduated Cylinder

Pipette

Spatula

Test tube

Tripod

This category is also available as outlines and silhouettes in the **Gallery** tab.

Sciences > Physics > Diagrams - Colour

Atomic Structure

Blackboard Formula

Magnet

Newton Cradle

Oscilloscope

Telescope

This category is also available as silhouettes in the **Gallery** tab.

Sports > Game Templates

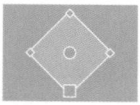

BasketBall Pitch

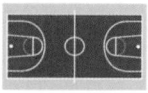

BasketBall Court

Chess Board

Cricket Pitch

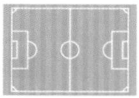

Football Pitch

Hockey Pitch

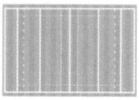

Rugby Pitch

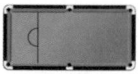

Snooker Table

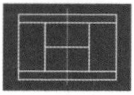

Tennis Clay Court

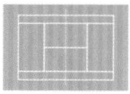

Tennis Grass Court

Sports > Sports Equipment

Bench

Dumbbell

Skip Rope

Stop Watch

Trampoline

Treadmill

Weights

Sports > Tactical Symbols

Central Line

Circle Marker

Cross Marker (small)

Cross Marker

Directional Sweep

Player Marker

Wing Arrow (down left)

Wing Arrow (down right)

Wing Arrow (up left)

Wing Arrow (up right)

x

X Marker (small)

X

X Marker

Badges

Badge 01

Badge 02

Badge 03

Badge 04

Badge 05

Badge 06

Badge 07

Badge 08

Badge 09

Badge 10

Banners

Banners 01

Banners 02

Banners 03

Banners 04

Banners 05

Banners 06

Banners 07

Banners 08

Banners 09

Banners 10

Embossed Shapes

Arrow 01

Arrow 02

Circle

Drop

Half Moon

Heart

Semi Circle

Speech Bubble

Splat

Square

Star

Triangle

Gel Shapes

Arrow

Ball

Button

Diamond

Droplet

Heart

Pill

Ring

Shield

Star

Tube

Shields

Shield 01

Shield 02

Shield 03

Shield 04

Shield 05

Shield 06

Shield 07

Shield 08

Shield 09

Shield 10

Splats

Scribble 01

Scribble 02

Scribble 03

Scribble 04

Scribble 05

Splat 01

Splat 02

Splat 03

Splat 04

Splat 05

Splat 06

Splat 07

Splodge 01

Splodge 02

Splodge 03

Splodge 04

Splodge 05

Splodge 06

Third Dimension

3D Shape 01

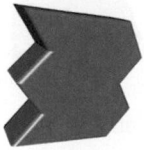
3D Shape 02

3D Shape 03

3D Shape 04

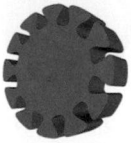
3D Shape 05

Third Dimension

3D Shape 06

3D Shape 07

3D Shape 08

3D Shape 09

3D Shape 10

3D Shape 11

3D Shape 12

3D Shape 13

3D Shape 14

3D Shape 15

3D Shape 16

3D Shape 17

3D Shape 18

3D Shape 19

3D Shape 20

3D Shape 21

3D Shape 22

3D Shape 23

3D Shape 24

3D Shape 25

3D Shape 26

3D Shape 27

3D Shape 28

3D Shape 29

3D Shape 30

Bright

Chat

Chat

Comment

Comment

Comment

Search

Cancel

Accept

Calendar

Shopping

Email

Home

Like

Tweet

Facebook

RSS

Portfolio

Photos

Document

Download

Back

Next

Up

Print

Button

Chat
Chat
Comment
Comment
Search
Cancel
Accept
Calendar
Shopping
Email
Home
Like
Tweet
Facebook
RSS
Portfolio
Document
Photos
Download
Back
Next
Up
Print

Dark Grey

Chat

Chat

Comment

Comment

Search

Cancel

Accept

Shopping

Calendar

Email

Home

Like

Tweet

Facebook

RSS

Portfolio

Document

Photos

Download

Back

Next

Up

Print

Standard

Chat

Chat

Comment

Comment

Comment

Search

Cancel

Accept

Calendar

Shopping

Email

Home

Like

Tweet

Facebook

RSS

Portfolio

Photos

Document

Download

Back

Next

Up

Print

Styles

The **Styles** tab contains multiple galleries of pre-designed styles that you can apply to any object, or customize to suit your own taste! When applied to an object, a style from the Styles tab will complement the object's other properties rather than replacing them.

The following categories are provided:

- 3D
- Bevels
- Blurs
- Edges
- Instant Effects
- Lines
- Presets - Default
- Shadows
- Stickers
- Text Effects
- Textures

The **Styles** tab also lets you store your own graphic styles in a **My Styles** section. This allows you to reuse them in any DrawPlus document.

Mixed

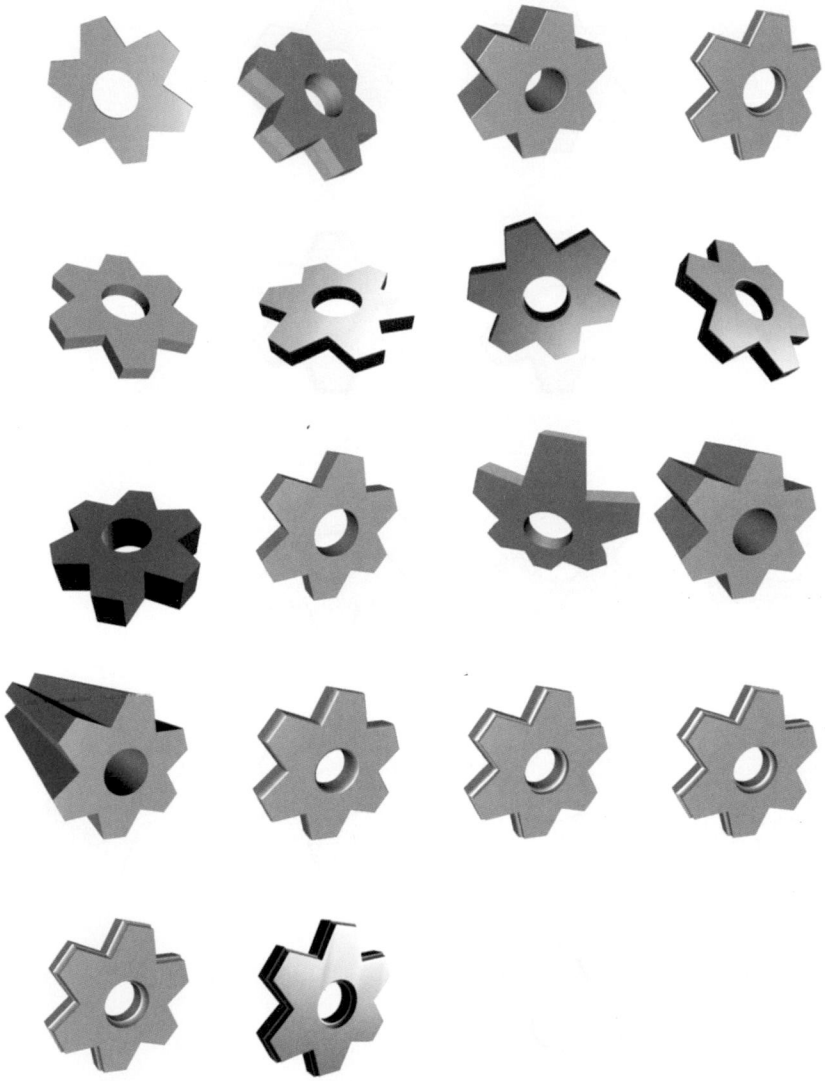

Inner Bevel

Emboss

Pillow

3D

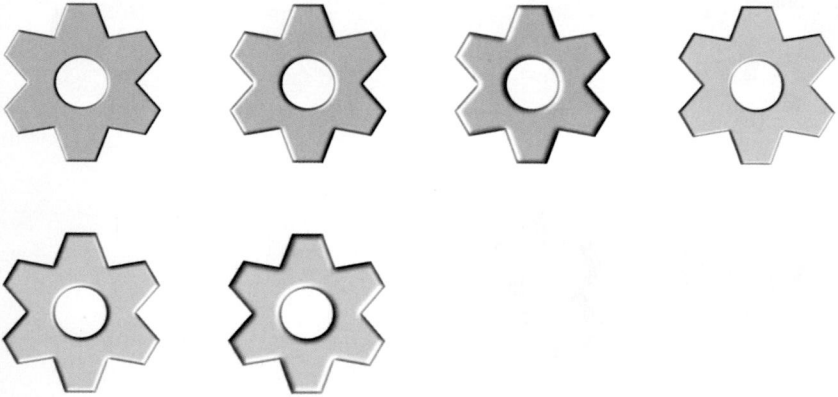

Gaussian

Radial

Zoom

Feathers

Glows

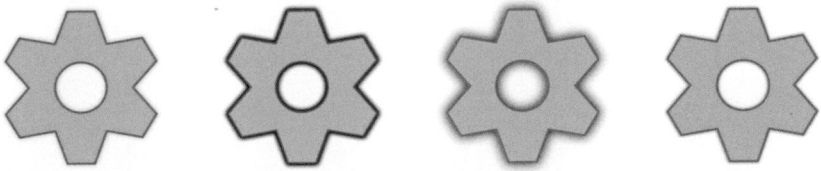

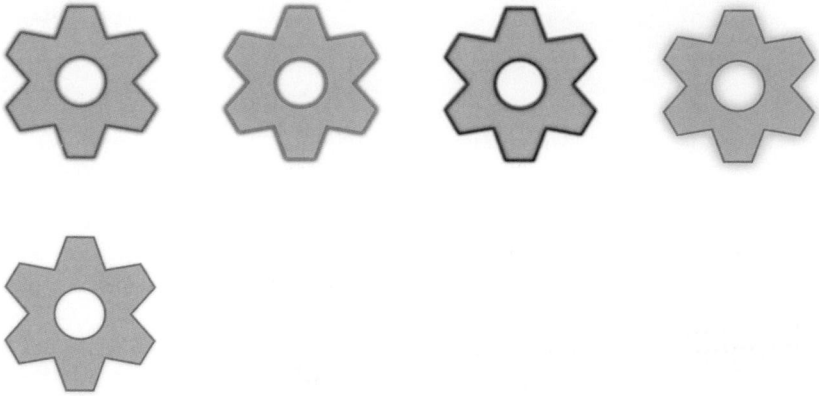

Paper

Animals

Edible

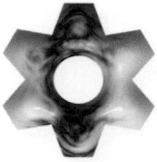
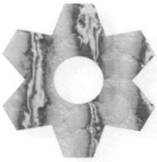

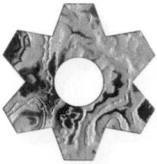

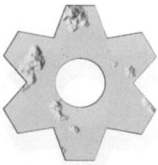

Elements

Glass

Glows

Gross

Marble

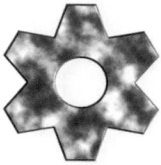

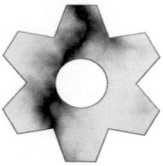
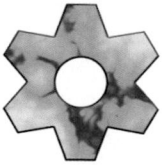

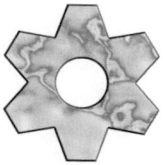
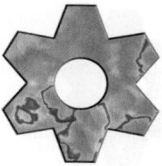

Metallic

Organic

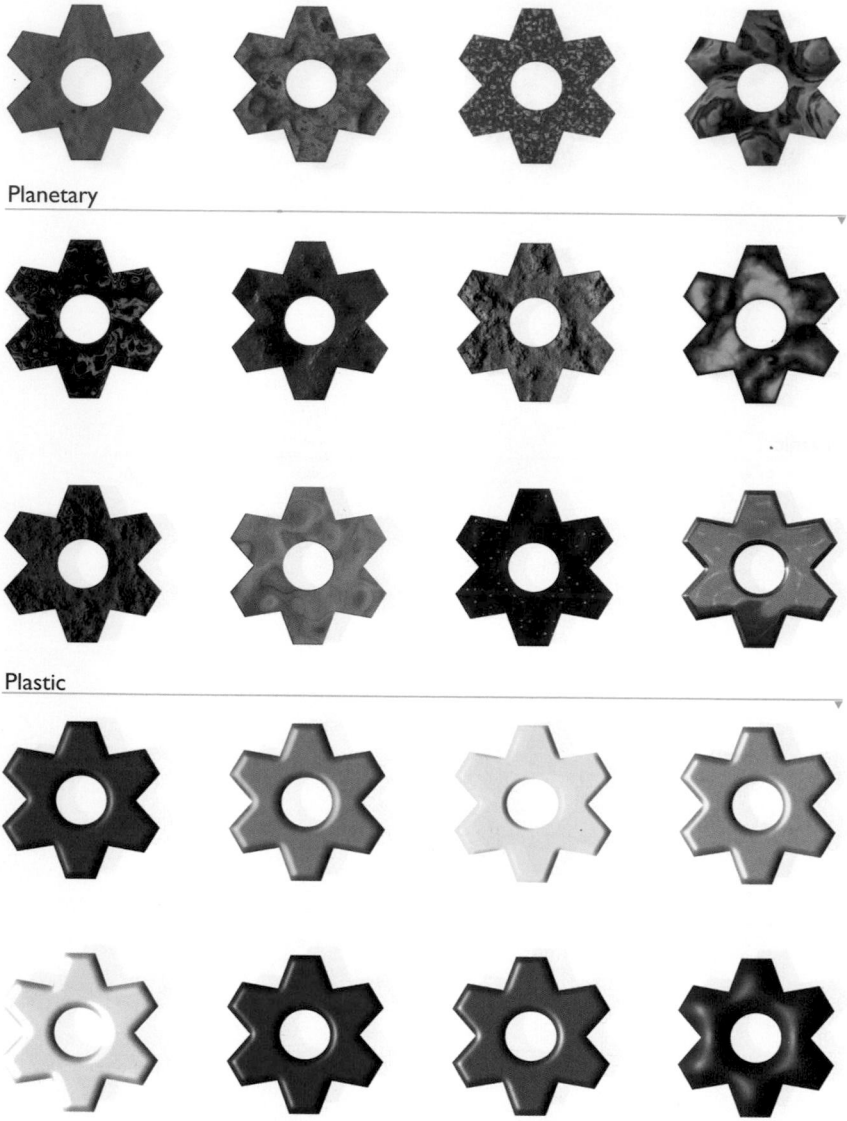
Planetary
Plastic

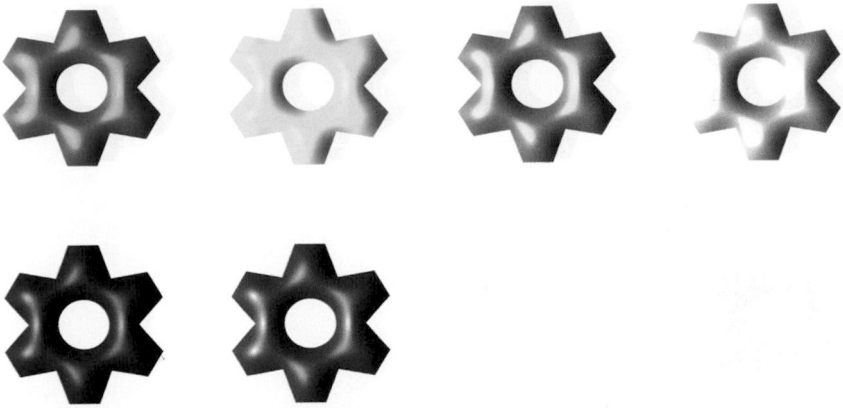

Stone

Wood

Lines

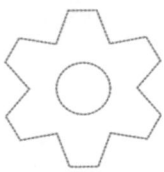

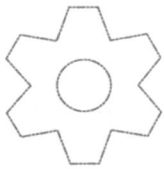
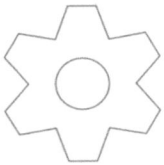

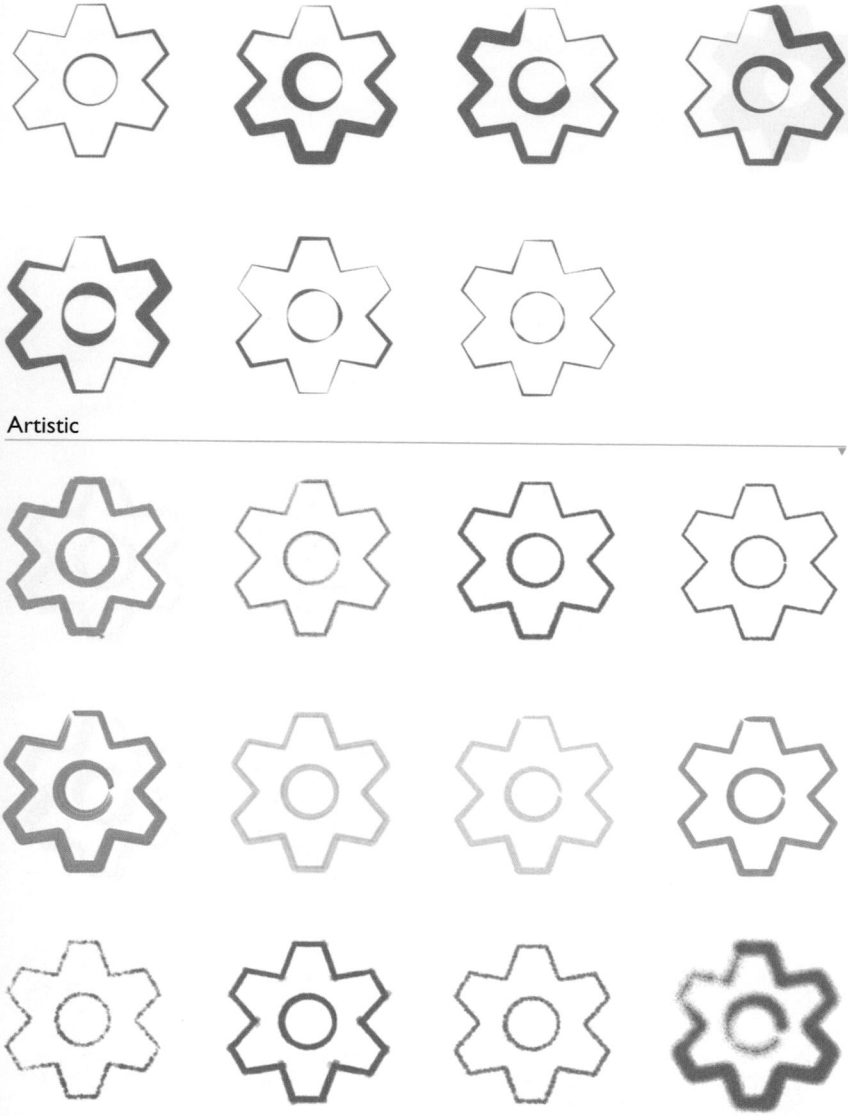
Artistic

Mixed

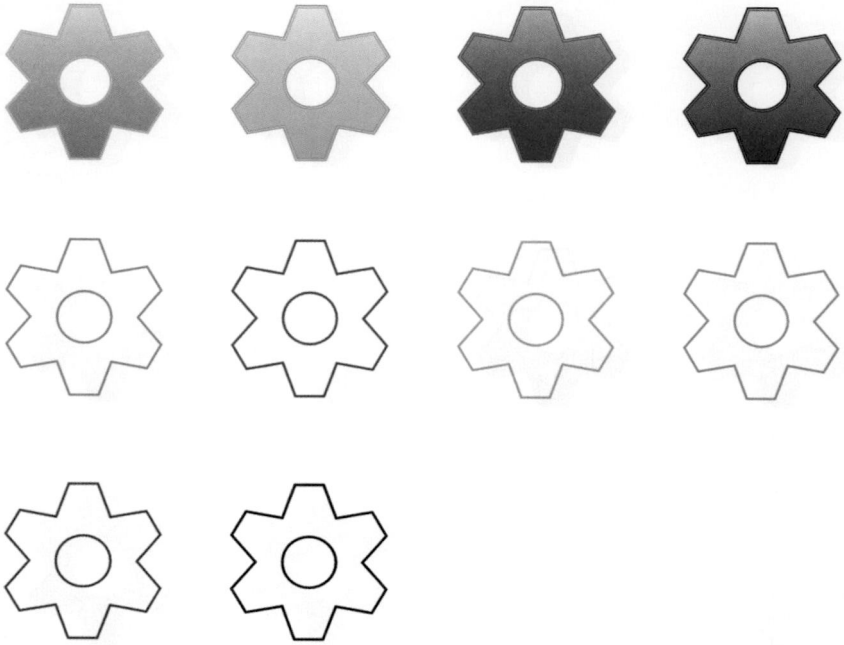

Drop Shadows

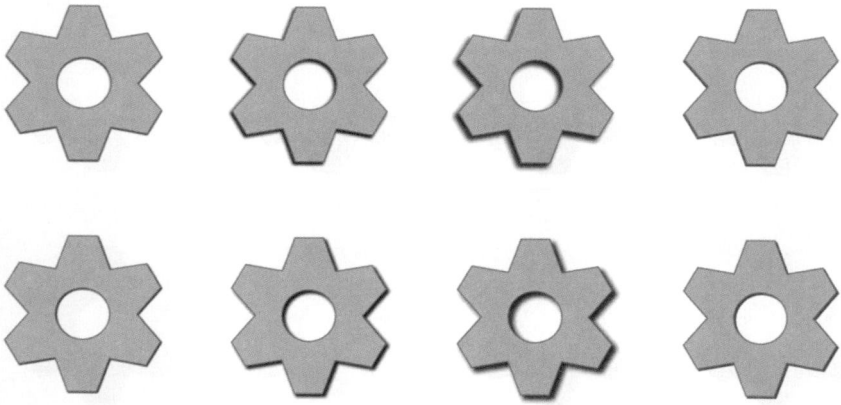

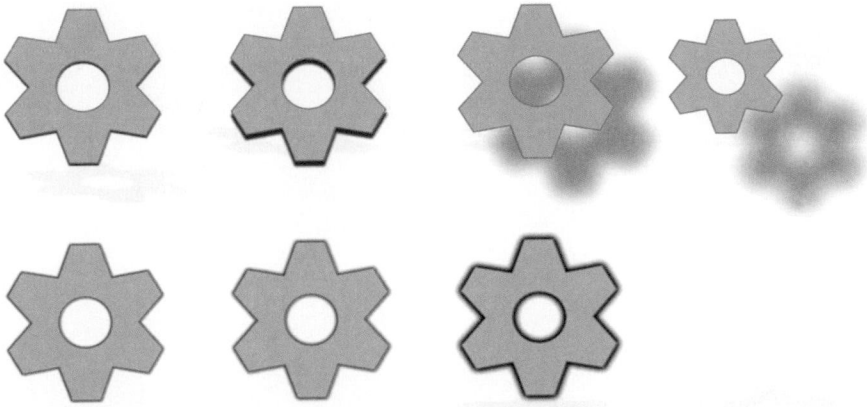

Inner Shadows

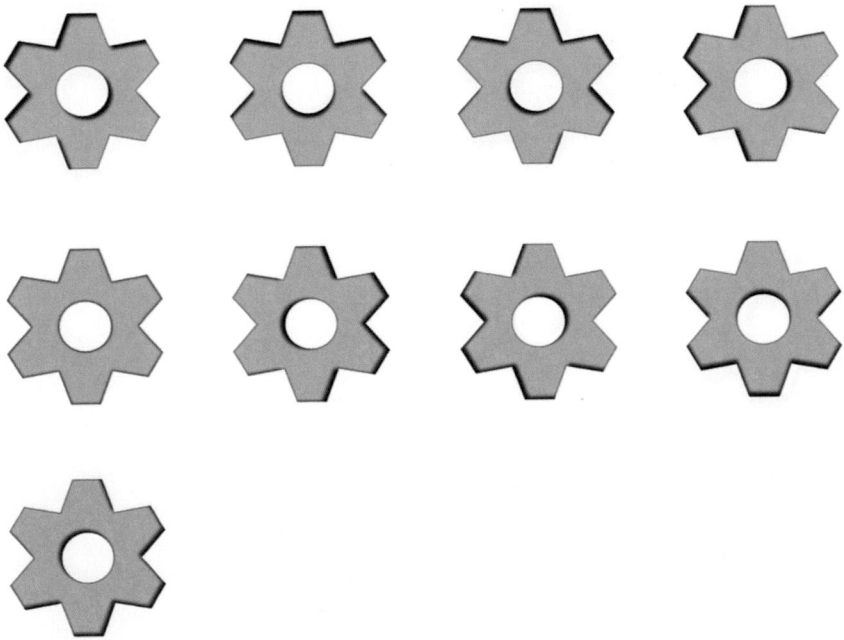

Perspective Shadows

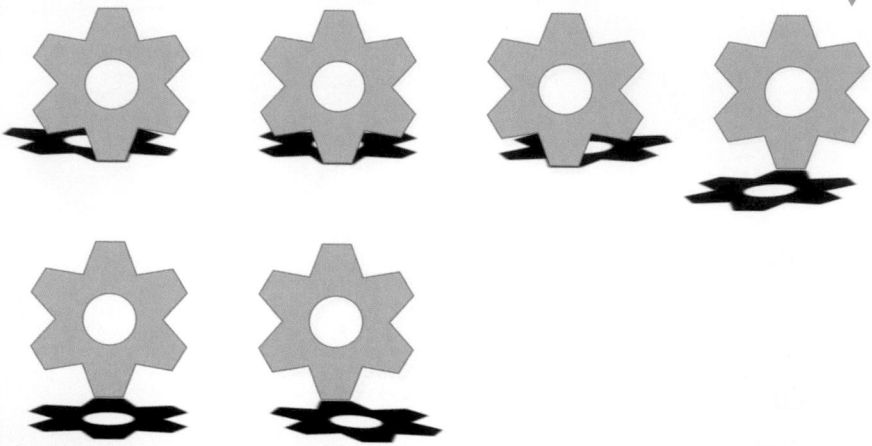

Stickers

Text Effects

Bump Maps

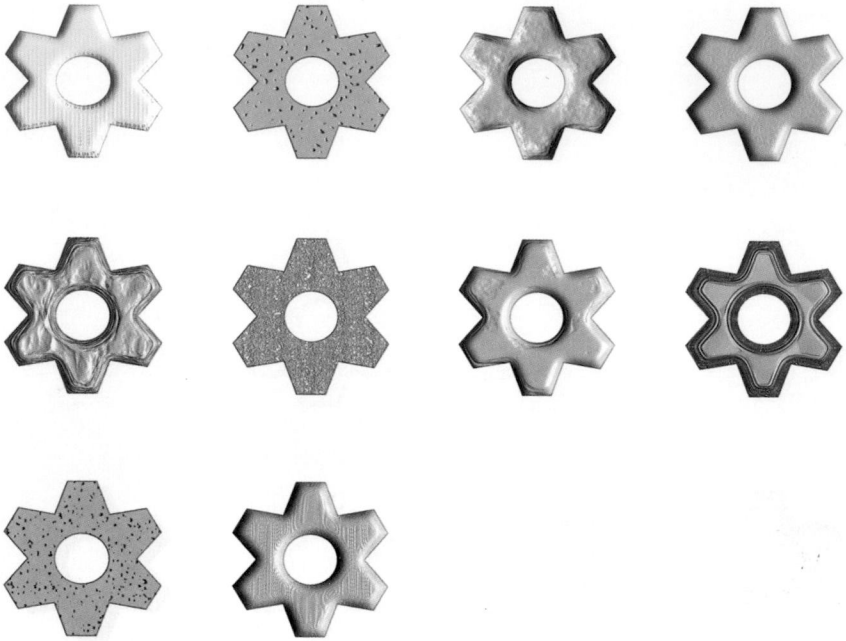

Brushes

DrawPlus provides an exciting and versatile range of brushes to be used in your digital artwork!

On the **Brushes** tab, you'll find a wide selection of brushes in the following categories:

- Draw
- Edges
- Effects
- Embroidery
- Grunge
- Nature
- Paint
- Photo
- Sponge
- Spray

Why not try these out with a graphics tablet and experiment with DrawPlus's **Pressure** tab functionality?

Chalk - Blunt

Chalk - Grainy

Chalk - Soft

Graphic Soft - Outline 01

Graphic Soft - Outline 02

Graphic Soft - Outline 03

Graphic Soft - Shading 01

Graphic Soft - Shading 02

Graphic Soft - Shading 03

Graphic Soft - Smudge 01

Graphic Soft - Smudge 02

Graphic Soft - Smudge 03

Marker Pen 01

Marker Pen 02

Marker Pen 03

Pen 01

Pen 02

Pen 03

Pen 04

Pencil 01

Pencil 02

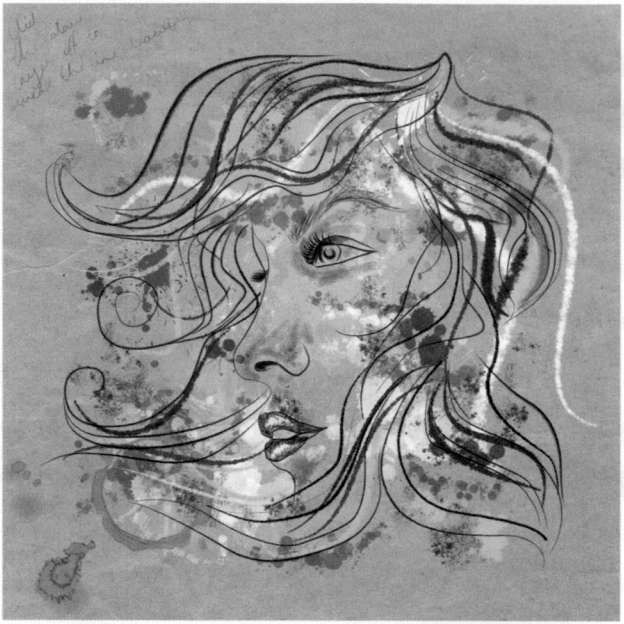

This sample, *Fashion Girl* was made using **Draw** and **Spray** brushes.

This sample, *Graphic Soft Pencil*, was made using the **Graphic Soft shading** brushes, which you'll find in the **Brushes** tab's **Draw** category.

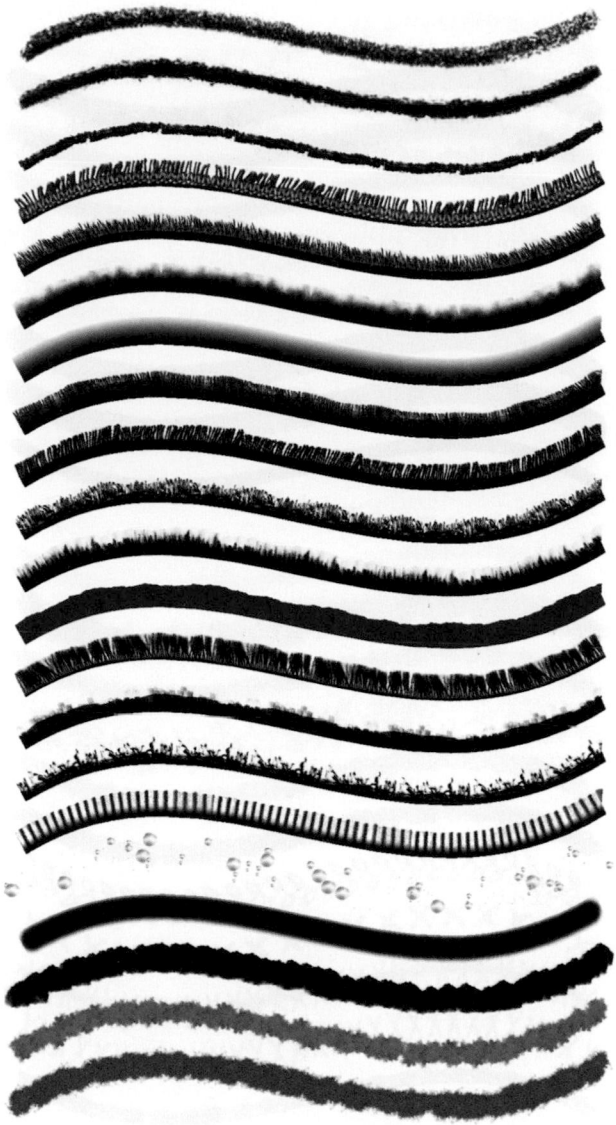
Pencil 03
Pencil 04
Burnt
Carpet
Denim
Felt
Glow
Hessian 01
Hessian 02
Messy
Painted
Ripped
Rug
Smudge
Splat
Stripes
Bubbles
Cartoon Outline
Clouds
Fire 01
Fire 02

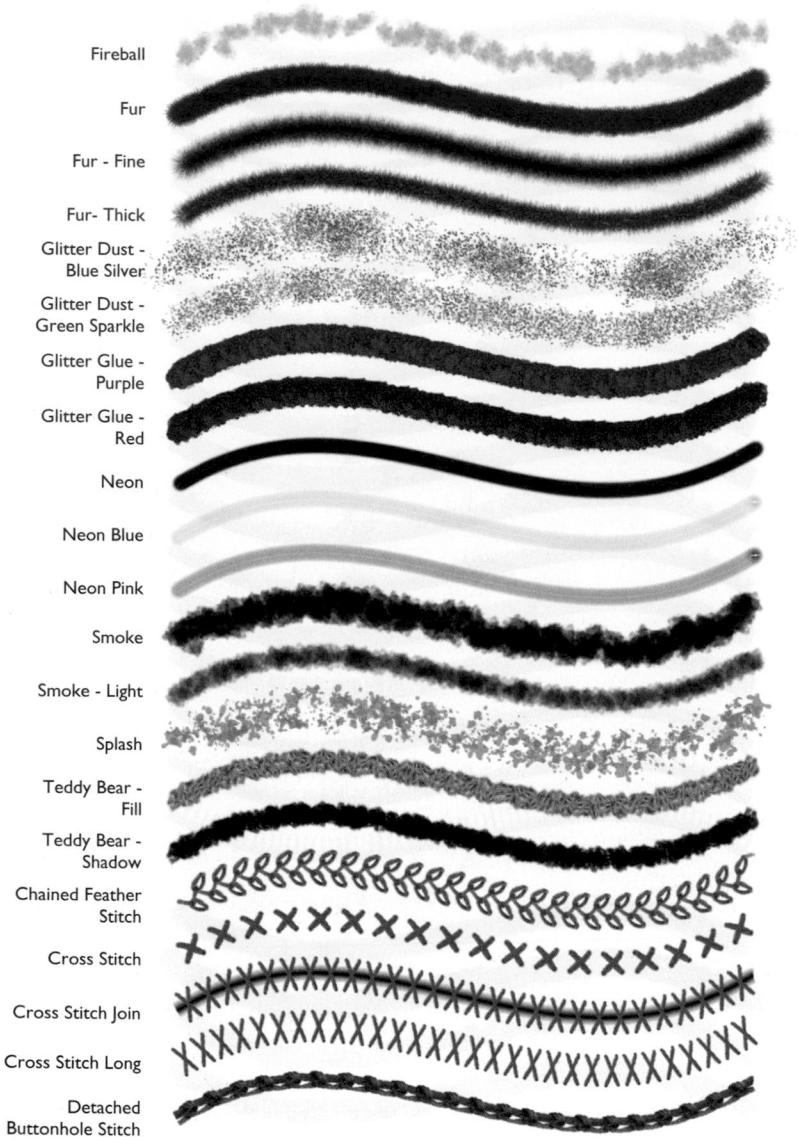
Fireball
Fur
Fur - Fine
Fur- Thick
Glitter Dust - Blue Silver
Glitter Dust - Green Sparkle
Glitter Glue - Purple
Glitter Glue - Red
Neon
Neon Blue
Neon Pink
Smoke
Smoke - Light
Splash
Teddy Bear - Fill
Teddy Bear - Shadow
Chained Feather Stitch
Cross Stitch
Cross Stitch Join
Cross Stitch Long
Detached Buttonhole Stitch

This sample, *Teddy Bear*, was made using the **Teddy Bear** brushes, located in the **Brushes** tab's **Effects** category.

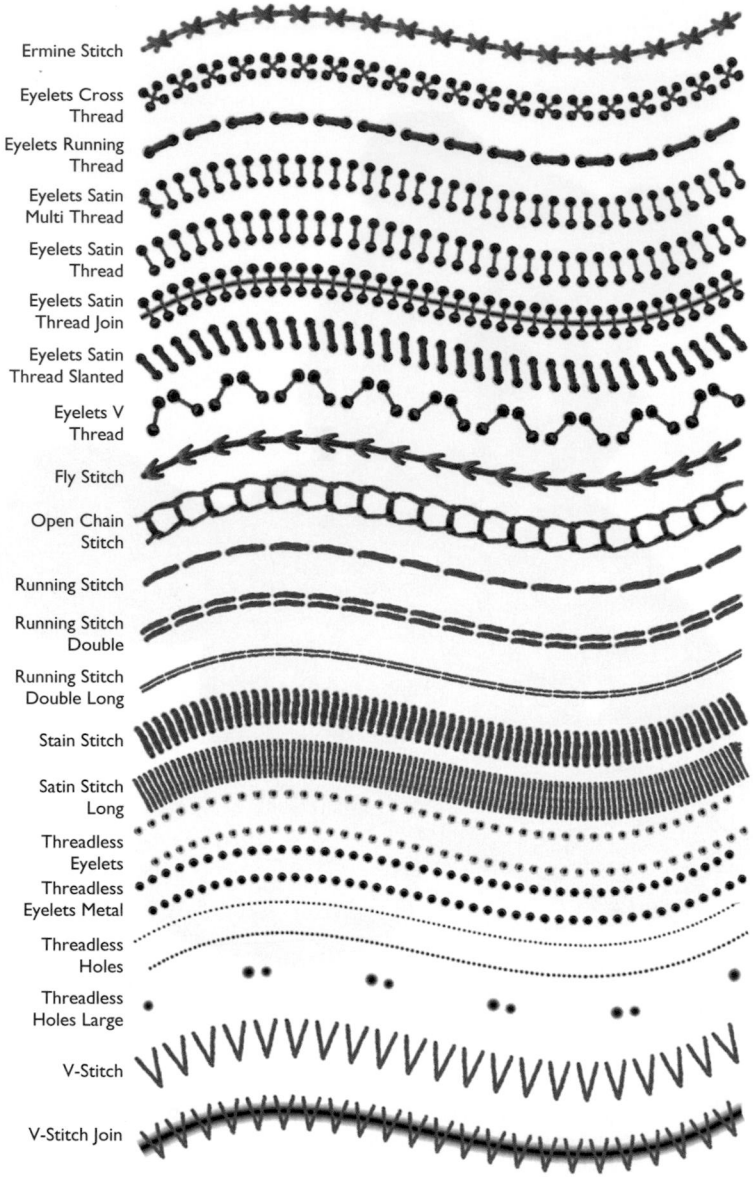
Ermine Stitch
Eyelets Cross Thread
Eyelets Running Thread
Eyelets Satin Multi Thread
Eyelets Satin Thread
Eyelets Satin Thread Join
Eyelets Satin Thread Slanted
Eyelets V Thread
Fly Stitch
Open Chain Stitch
Running Stitch
Running Stitch Double
Running Stitch Double Long
Stain Stitch
Satin Stitch Long
Threadless Eyelets
Threadless Eyelets Metal
Threadless Holes
Threadless Holes Large
V-Stitch
V-Stitch Join

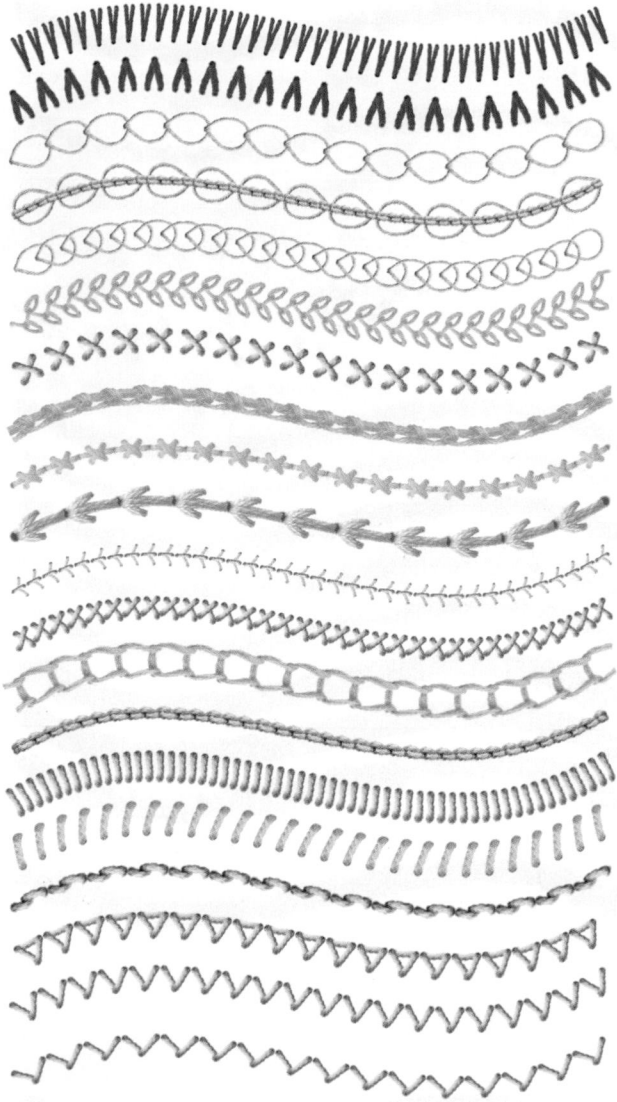

V-Stitch Long

V-Stitch Reverse

White Chain Stitch

White Chain Stitch Outline

White Chain Stitch Short

White Chained Feather Stitch

White Cross Stitch

White Detached Buttonhole Stitch

White Ermine Stitch

White Fly Stitch

White Fly Stitch Small

White Herringbone Stitch

White Open Chain Stitch

White Outline Stitch

White Satin Stitch

White Satin Stitch Slanted

White Stem Stitch

White Tri Stitch

White V-Stitch

White V-Stitch Wide

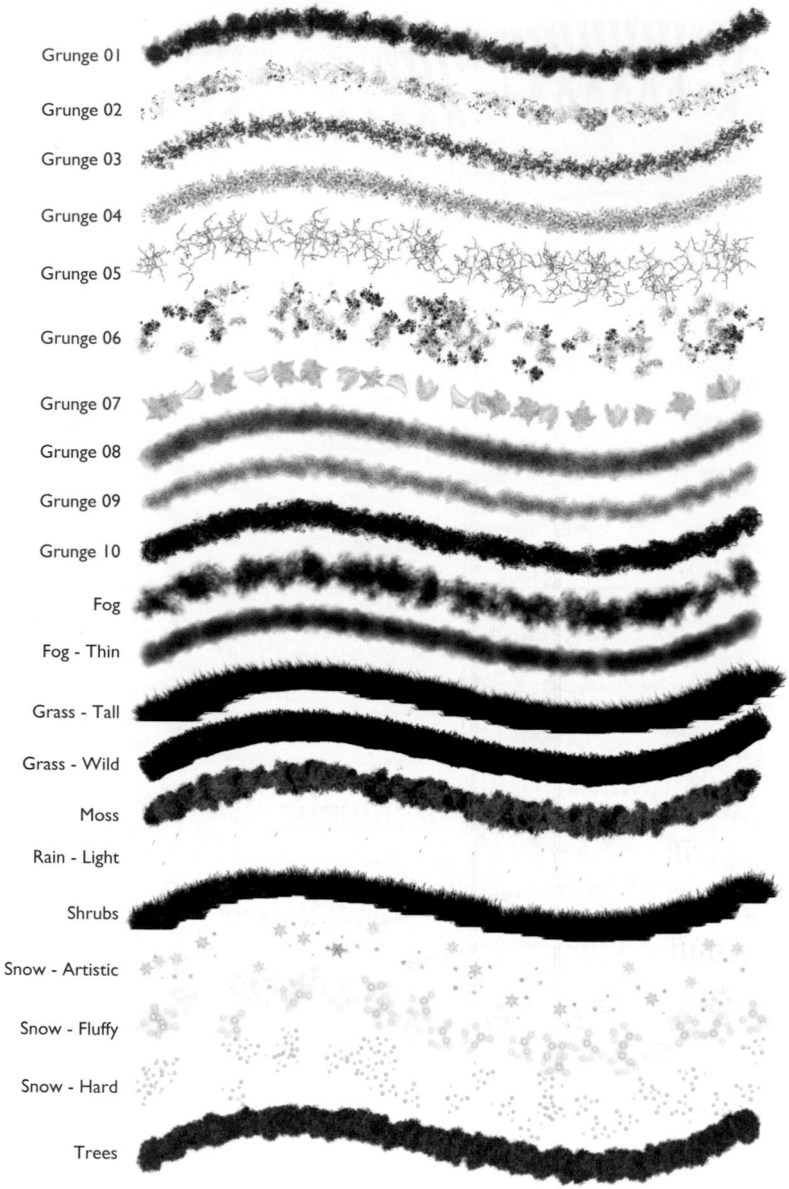
Grunge 01
Grunge 02
Grunge 03
Grunge 04
Grunge 05
Grunge 06
Grunge 07
Grunge 08
Grunge 09
Grunge 10
Fog
Fog - Thin
Grass - Tall
Grass - Wild
Moss
Rain - Light
Shrubs
Snow - Artistic
Snow - Fluffy
Snow - Hard
Trees

This sample, *Cloudy Night*, was made using the **Tree** and **Fog** brushes, located in the **Brushes** tab's **Nature** category.

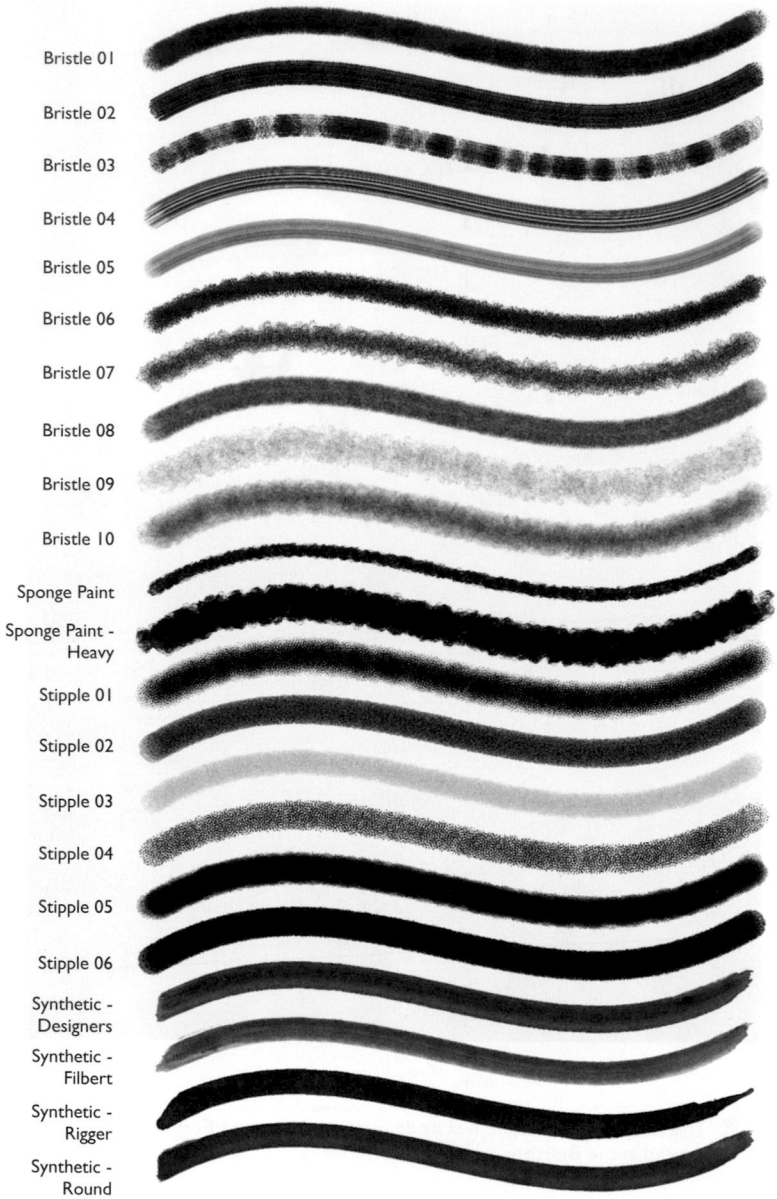
Bristle 01
Bristle 02
Bristle 03
Bristle 04
Bristle 05
Bristle 06
Bristle 07
Bristle 08
Bristle 09
Bristle 10
Sponge Paint
Sponge Paint - Heavy
Stipple 01
Stipple 02
Stipple 03
Stipple 04
Stipple 05
Stipple 06
Synthetic - Designers
Synthetic - Filbert
Synthetic - Rigger
Synthetic - Round

Synthetic - Wash

Wash - Fine

Wash - Heavy

Wash - Jitter

Wash - Loose

Wash - Mop

Wash - Oval

Wash - Round

Beads

Candy

Chain

Confetti

Grass

Grass Cuttings

Jewels

Pencil Shavings

Purple Flowers

Rope - Thick

Rope - Thin

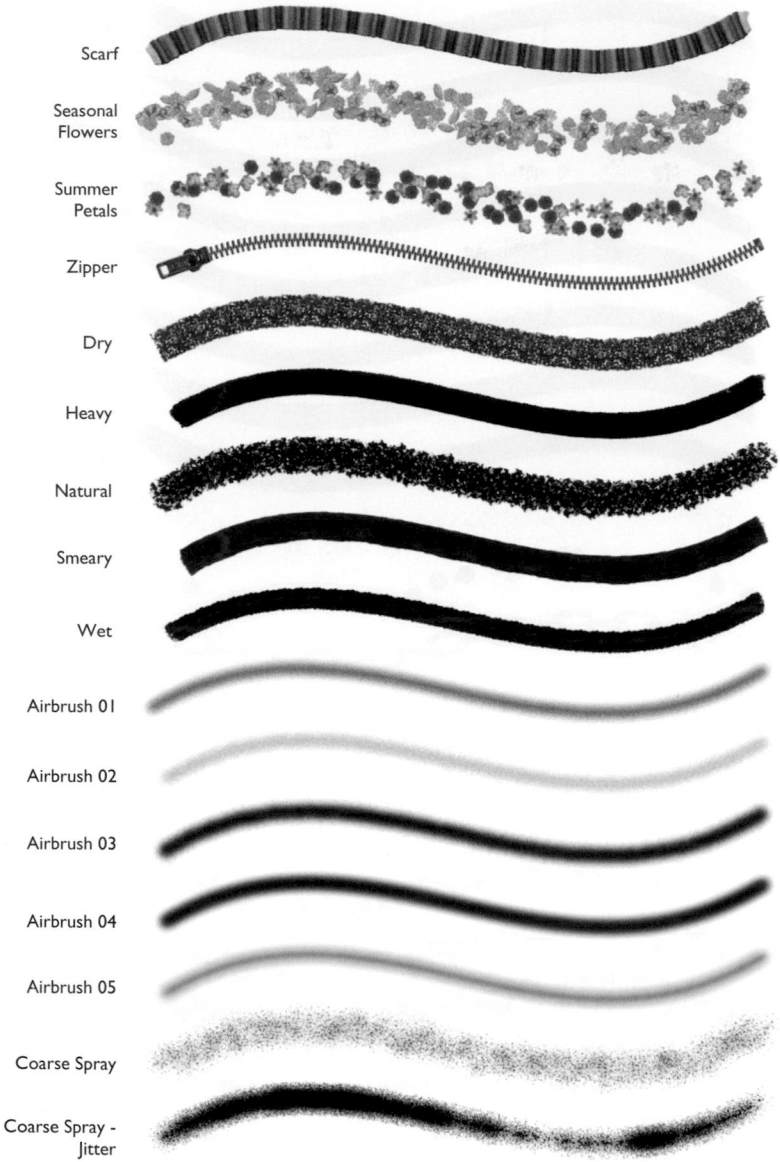
Scarf
Seasonal Flowers
Summer Petals
Zipper
Dry
Heavy
Natural
Smeary
Wet
Airbrush 01
Airbrush 02
Airbrush 03
Airbrush 04
Airbrush 05
Coarse Spray
Coarse Spray - Jitter

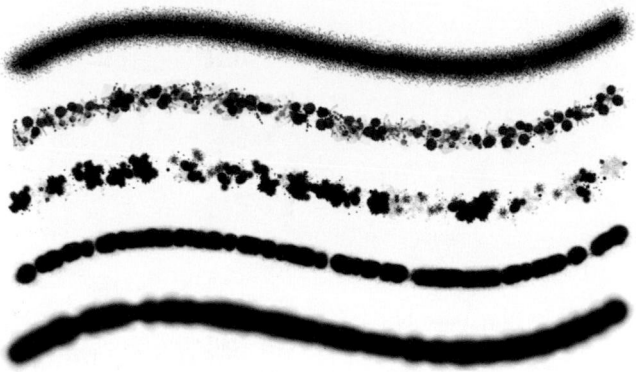

Coarse Spray-Medium

Splats 01

Splats 02

Spray Can 01

Spray Can 02

Samples

DrawPlus X5 comes with a varied selection of samples, showcasing the possibilities for your own artistic creations.

Whether your looking for inspiration for your own **digital art, illustration**, **print project** or **animation**, the DrawPlus samples are a one-stop-shop for ideas!

Efrain Hernandez : Out Of This

Efrain Hernandez : Geisha

Ken Cope : African Elephant

New to X5! Check out our *Featured Users* section—showcasing some of our DrawPlus users excellent work!

Cherry Blossom

The *Cherry Blossom* sample was created using the **Erase** and **Multiply blend modes.**

Cloudy Night

Fashion Girl

Fireball

The *Fireball* sample was created using the **Fireball** and **Smoke** brushes, found in the **Effects** section in the **Brushes** tab.

Graphic Soft Pencil

The *Graphic Soft Pencil* sample was created with the **Graphic Soft Shading** brushes, found in the **Draw** section in the **Brushes** tab.

Portrait

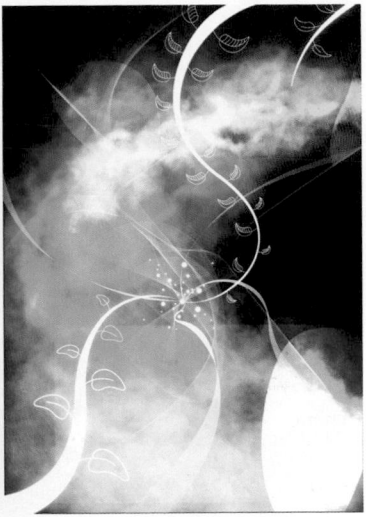

Vision

Teddy Bear

The *Teddy Bear* sample was created using the **Teddy Bear Fill / Shadow** brushes, found in the **Effects** section in the **Brushes** tab.

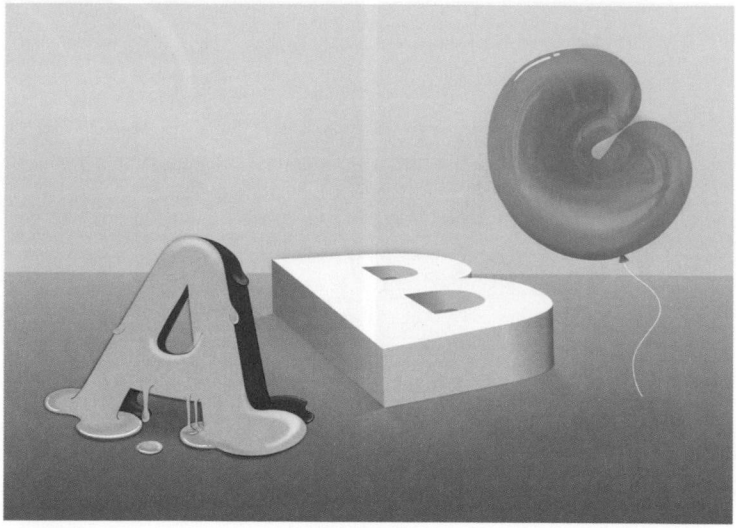

ABC

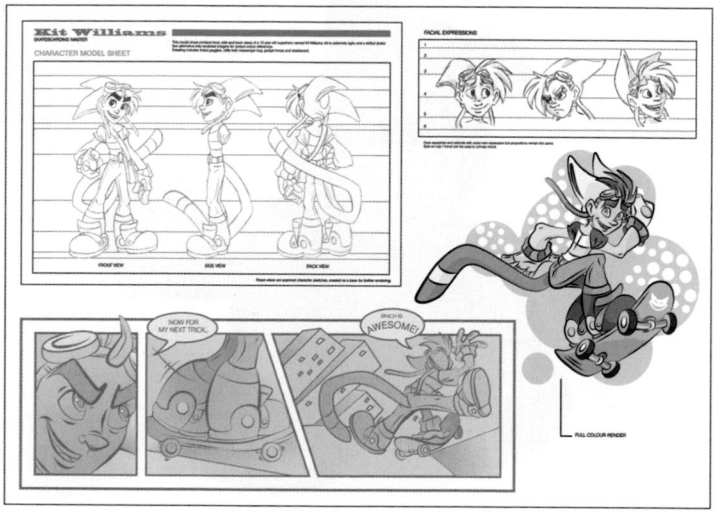

Character Sheet

Dog

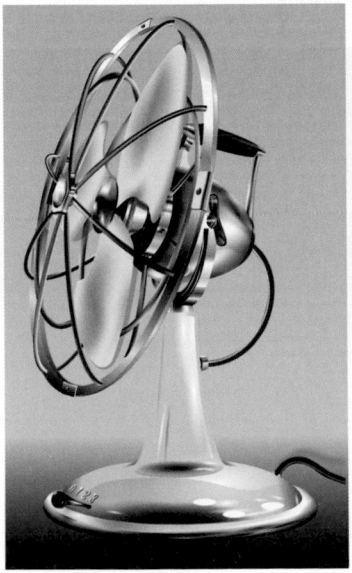

Electric Fan

Electricity

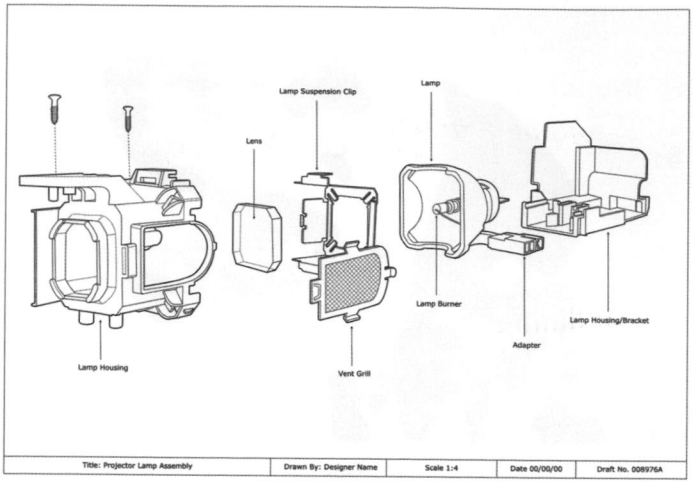

Exploded Drawing

Space Boys

Manga

The *Manga* sample was created using **pressure sensitivity** and a **graphics tablet**.

Sports Car

Tyre

World Window

Watch

Balanced Diet

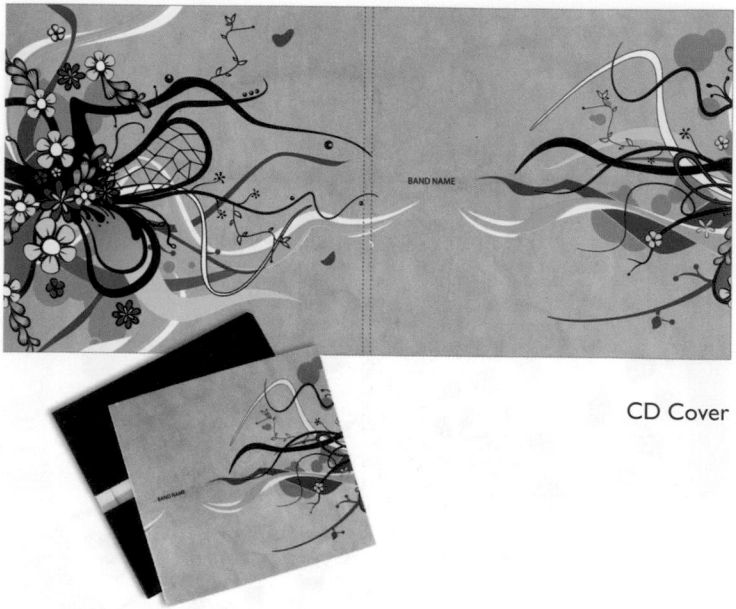

CD Cover

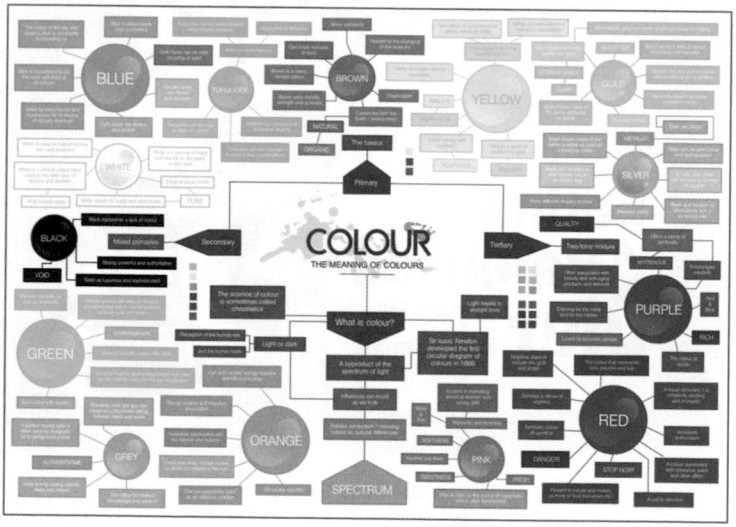

Colour Flowchart

Country Folk

Dinosaur

The *Dinosaur* typography sample was made using **Artistic Text** and **Preset Text Paths.**

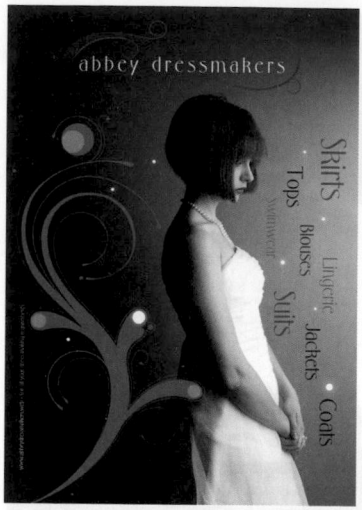

Dressmakers

Juicebox

Logo

Mixed Media

The *Mixed Media* sample shows what you can achieve using multiple tools in DrawPlus!

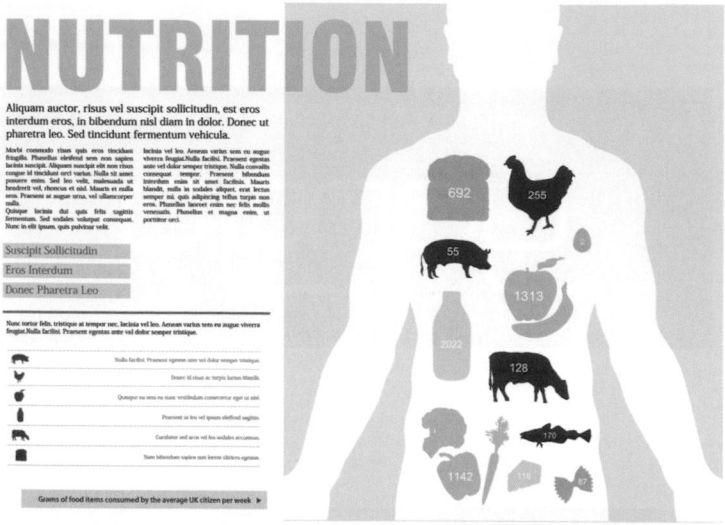

Nutrition

Organic Cosmetics

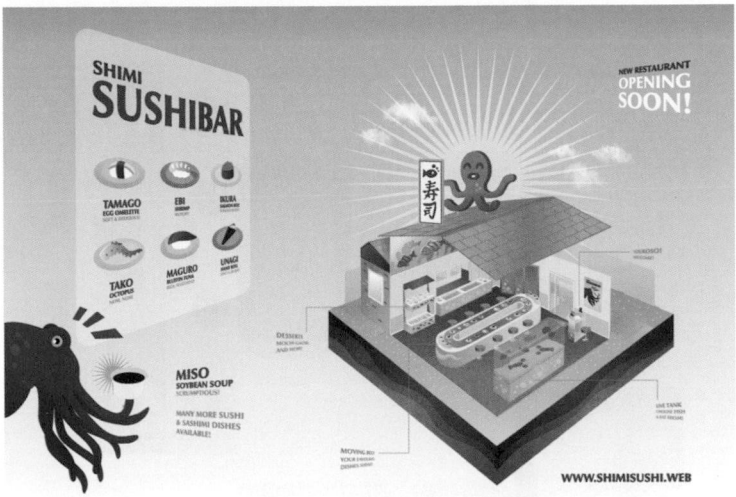

Sushi Bar

Village Fair

Sushi Bar and *Village Fair* samples are both **Vector** drawings created using the **Pen Tool**. *Sushi Bar* also utilises the **Perspective Tool**!

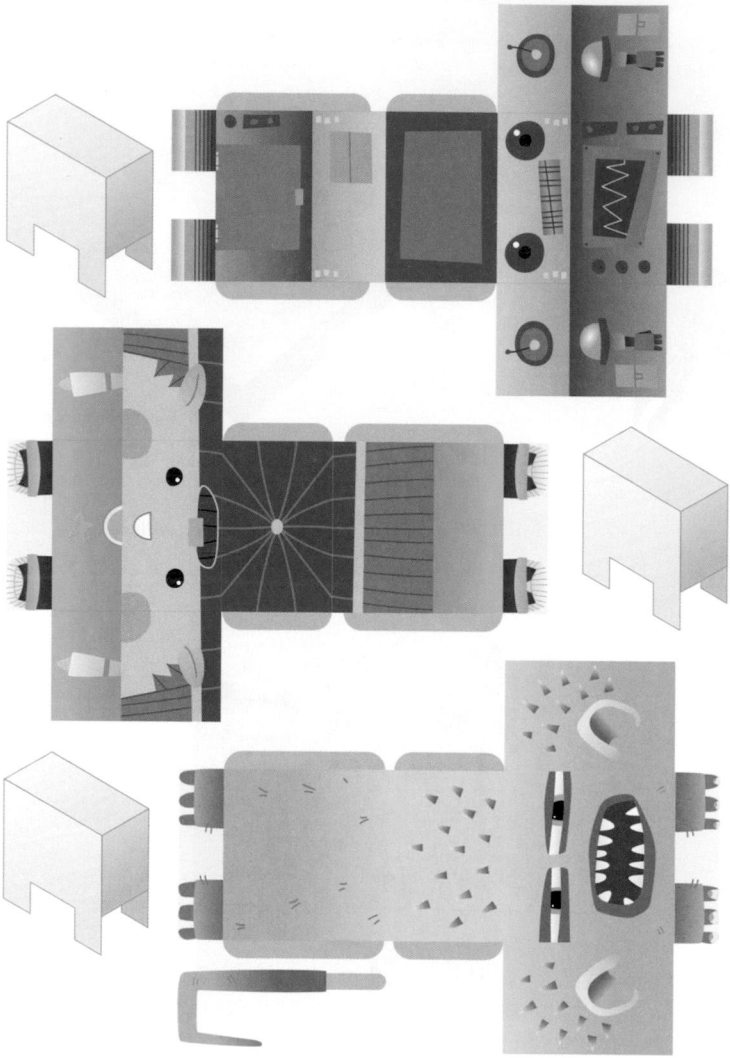

Box Toys

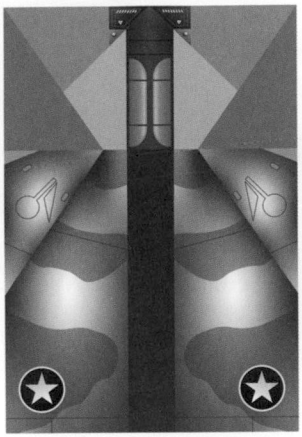

Jet Plane

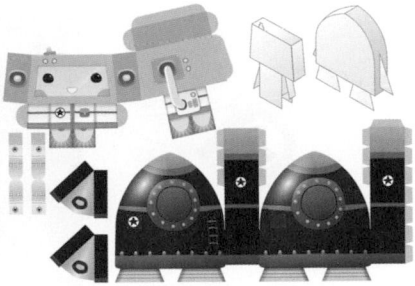

Space Toy

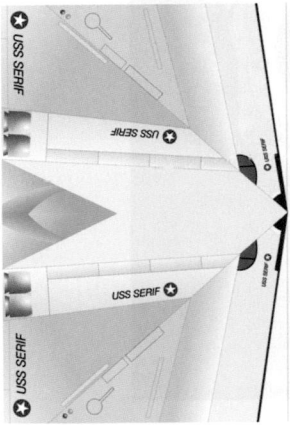

Shuttle

Headphones PopUp Card

Fish

Fun Frogs

Watch